First World War
and Army of Occupation
War Diary
France, Belgium and Germany

2 DIVISION
19 Infantry Brigade,
Brigade Train
22 August 1914 - 30 November 1914

WO95/1367/2

The Naval & Military Press Ltd
www.nmarchive.com
Published in association with The National Archives

Published by

The Naval & Military Press Ltd

Unit 10 Ridgewood Industrial Park,

Uckfield, East Sussex,

TN22 5QE England

Tel: +44 (0) 1825 749494

www.naval-military-press.com

www.nmarchive.com

This diary has been reprinted in facsimile from the original. Any imperfections are inevitably reproduced and the quality may fall short of modern type and cartographic standards.

© **Crown Copyright**
Images reproduced by permission of The National Archives, London, England, 2015.

Contents

Document type	Place/Title	Date From	Date To
Heading	WO95/1367 Brigade Train		
Heading	2 Division 19 Brigade Train 1914 Aug-1915 Aug		
Heading	19th Infantry Brigade Train August 1914.		
Heading	War Diary of 19th Infantry Brigade Train August 22-1914 To Aug 31, 1914		
War Diary	Amiens	22/08/1914	22/08/1914
War Diary	Valenciennes	23/08/1914	23/08/1914
War Diary	Quievrechain	24/08/1914	24/08/1914
War Diary	Jenlain	25/08/1914	25/08/1914
War Diary	Le Cateau	26/08/1914	26/08/1914
War Diary	St. Quentin	26/08/1914	26/08/1914
War Diary	Noyon	27/08/1914	28/08/1914
War Diary	Pontoise	29/08/1914	29/08/1914
War Diary	Carlepont	30/08/1914	30/08/1914
War Diary	Couloisy	31/08/1914	31/08/1914
Heading	Train 19th Infantry Brigade September 1914		
War Diary	Saintimes Baron	01/09/1914	01/09/1914
War Diary	Dammartin	02/09/1914	02/09/1914
War Diary	Lagny	03/09/1914	03/09/1914
War Diary	Bois De Chigny	04/09/1914	04/09/1914
War Diary	Brie Comte Robert	05/09/1914	05/09/1914
War Diary	Grisy	06/09/1914	06/09/1914
War Diary	Villeneuve St Denis	07/09/1914	07/09/1914
War Diary	Villers Sur Morin	08/09/1914	08/09/1914
War Diary	Pierre Levee	09/09/1914	09/09/1914
War Diary	Jouarre	10/09/1914	10/09/1914
War Diary	East Of Cocherez	11/09/1914	11/09/1914
War Diary	Marizy St Genevieve	12/09/1914	12/09/1914
War Diary	Villers Helon	13/09/1914	13/09/1914
War Diary	Le Carriere L'Eveque	14/09/1914	14/09/1914
War Diary	Septmonts	15/09/1914	30/09/1914
Heading	War Diary of O.C. 19th Infantry Brigade Train From 1/9/14 To 30/9/14 Volume II		
Heading	19th Infantry Brigade October 1914.		
Heading	19th Brigade Train Vol III 1-31.10.14		
War Diary	Septmonts	01/10/1914	05/10/1914
War Diary	St. Remy	06/10/1914	06/10/1914
War Diary	Vez	07/10/1914	07/10/1914
War Diary	Pont Maxence	08/10/1914	08/10/1914
War Diary	Estrees. St. Denis	09/10/1914	09/10/1914
War Diary	Watten	10/10/1914	10/10/1914
War Diary	St. Omer	11/10/1914	11/10/1914
War Diary	Borre	12/10/1914	12/10/1914
War Diary	One Mile North Borre	13/10/1914	13/10/1914
War Diary	Bailleul	14/10/1914	15/10/1914
War Diary	Vlamertinghe	16/10/1914	19/10/1914
War Diary	Laventie	20/10/1914	20/10/1914
War Diary	Sailly Sur Lys	21/10/1914	31/10/1914
Heading	Train 19th Infantry Brigade November 1914.		
Heading	19th Brigade Train Vol IV 1-30.11.14		

Type	Location	From	To
War Diary	Sailly Sur Lys.	01/11/1914	16/11/1914
War Diary	Nieppe (Near) (Les Trois. Tilleuls)	17/11/1914	30/11/1914
Heading	Train 19th Infantry Brigade December 1914.		
Heading	19th Brigade Train Vol V 1-31.12.14		
War Diary	Les Trois. Tilleuls (near Pont De Nieppe)	01/12/1914	10/12/1914
War Diary	Les 3 Tilleuls France	11/12/1914	31/12/1914
Heading	19th Brigade Train Vol VI 1-31.1.16		
War Diary	Les 3 Tilleuls France	01/01/1915	31/01/1915
Heading	19th Brigade Train Vol VII 1-28.2.15		
War Diary	Les 3 Tilleuls, France	01/02/1915	28/02/1915
Heading	XIX Infantry Brigade. Train Vol VIII 1-31.3.15		
War Diary	Les 3 Tilleuls France	01/03/1915	31/03/1915
Heading	19th Brigade Train Vol IX 1-30.4.15		
War Diary	Les 3 Tilleuls France	01/04/1915	30/04/1915
Heading	19th Bde Train Vol X		
War Diary	Les 3 Tilleuls France	01/05/1915	02/05/1915
War Diary	Erquinghem-Lys	03/05/1915	31/05/1915
Heading	27th Division 19th Infy Bde 19th Bde Train A.S.C. Jun-Jly 1915		
Heading	19th Brigade 19th Bde: Train Vol XI		
War Diary	Erquinghem-Lys	01/06/1915	30/06/1915
Heading	19th Brigade 19th Bde Train Vol XII		
War Diary	Erquinghem-Lys	01/07/1915	15/07/1915
War Diary	Steenwerck	16/07/1915	21/07/1915
War Diary	Doulieu	22/07/1915	31/07/1915
Heading	(Became No. 2 Coy. 2nd Divisional Train 19.8.15) War Diary 19th Infantry Brigade Train. August 1915 (1.8.15-19.8.15)		
War Diary	Doulieu France	01/08/1915	05/08/1915
War Diary	Doulieu	05/08/1915	19/08/1915
Heading	Reserve Brigade Train October & November 1914		
Heading	Reserve Brigade Train Vol I 14.10-30.11.14		
Heading	War Diary-Period (a) 14 October 31st October 1914 (b) 1st November to 30th November.		
War Diary	Le Boisle	14/10/1914	14/10/1914
War Diary	Stomer	15/10/1914	30/11/1914

WO 95/1867
Brigade Train

2 DIVISION

19 BRIGADE

BRIGADE TRAIN

1914 AUG — 1915 AUG

19th Infantry Brigade.

19th INFANTRY BRIGADE

TRAIN

AUGUST 1914.

Volume I.

Confidential

121/868

War Diary
of
19th. Infantry Brigade TRAIN.

August 22-1914. To Aug. 31. 1914.

War Diary

Hour	Date	Place	Summary of Events & Information	Remarks & references to appendices
	Sept			

19th Infantry Brigade TRAIN.

AUGUST = 1914.

Army Form C. 2118.

WAR DIARY
of 19th Infy. Brigade Train.

INTELLIGENCE SUMMARY. by

(Erase heading not required.)

Instructions regarding War Diaries and Intelligence Summaries are contained in F.S. Regs., Part II. and the Staff Manual respectively. Title pages will be prepared in manuscript.

Hour, Date, Place	Summary of Events and Information	Remarks and references to Appendices
	DIARY written BY X 19th Infantry Brigade TRAIN. (Capt. A. Clifton-Shellin A.S.C.)	
August 22nd 1914: AMIENS.	Reported to A.D.J.T. on arrival from LE HAVRE & received instructions on formation of Train for newly formed 19th Brigade. Orders to de-train A.S.C. personnel & at VALENCIENNES.	
" 23rd ... VALENCIENNES 1.30 a.m.	Arrived @ VALENCIENNES at 1.30 a.m. Detrained A.S.C. personnel & 3 Reserves. Orders at 3 P.m. from Brigade Hd. to proceed to QUIEVRECHAIN – At that place filled from Supply Column —	
" 24th ... QUIEVRECHAIN 12.3 a.m.	Received orders (at 12.3 a.m.) to proceed with TRAIN to ATHIS via QUIEVRANT and ELOUGES. — By 12.30 a.m. — Near ATHIS Train came under Shell fire* & had to put escort into Wagons to avoid Conflict. Had orders to wait	*x "Trains being forbidden to remain at ATHIS I'm stood proceed to ROISIN and await orders there" SD F.P. Dunlop Capt. D.A.D.T. 19th Div." See Appendices ATHIS 8.50 a.m.
6.50 a.m. at ATHIS	at ATHIS but at 8.50 a.m. a Staff Officer gave me an order to move to MONS to ROISIN – Owing to proximity of fighting – At 10.30 a.m. Fug. S.O. sent message to ROISIN to order Train to PRESSAU via VILLERS POL. Learnt from Enquiries that 19th Brigade was at JENLAIN & in absence of orders processed there.	Owing to Mis Circular March 8 the absence of orders from Brigade Hd. it was impossible to fill Train.
6 p.m.		
" 25th ... JENLAIN 1.50 a.m.	Orders to march to HAUSSY, and be clear of Rail Junc: LE QUESNOY MAING by 5.30 a.m. — Actually clear by 4.30 a.m. — After leaving BERMERN Stopped and	

(9 29 6) W 3352—1107 100,000 10/13 H W V Forms/C.2118/M.

WAR DIARY or INTELLIGENCE SUMMARY.

Army Form C. 2118.

(Erase heading not required.)

Hour, Date, Place	Summary of Events and Information	Remarks and references to Appendices
LE CATEAU 26th August	Questioned flying French Cavalrymen & fugitive civilians & learnt Enemy were at HASPRES. Before reaching HAUSSY a body of German Cavalry opened a sharp fire on train to which we replied. × Reaching HAUSSY the Post Authorities informed me the French authorities had ordered the Post Office to be closed & the Mairie orders everyone to leave the Town. As the Germans were pressing on, I decided to move train to SOLESMES. There I interviewed the park and obtain orders – but ½ hour after arrival the Commandant d'Armes motored up & ordered me to leave the Town; also he said the Germans were entering the Town. – I decided to go to LE CATEAU, in which direction I saw British Troops moving. – I then went & reported to Army Headquarters and reported that the Germans were on the line HASPRES – HAUSSY – SOLESMES. I got into touch with Supply Column at midnight & filled body on the 26th August. – Ordered to march at 4.15 a.m. to ESTRÉES via MARETZ. – Moved off, actually, at 3.30 a.m. – Halted at ESTRÉES at 1.30 a.m. Orders were passed on from 5th Divisional Train to move on towards ST QUENTIN. – It was reported that enemy were close upon us & stand parties were thrown out for train protection. – Halted Train 2½ miles N. of ST QUENTIN to water & feed & proceeded to ST QUENTIN myself for orders. – G.H.Q. having moved I got no definite information. 6.30 a.m. – station. I decided as it was dusk to bring train into ST QUENTIN	× One of our riding horses got away during this little fight & has been reported missing. –

War Diary

19th Infantry Brigade Train

Hour Date Place	Summary of Events & Information	Remarks & references to appendices
27th Aug. 5.30 a.m. ST. QUENTIN	There, whilst I was endeavouring to get into touch with Headquarters — General Sir H. Smith-Dorrien arrived and informed him of the situation and that I had no orders. — On hearing from me that G.H.Q. had gone to NOYON he gave me an Order to take Train to NOYON — Jarcendingh marched there and arrived at 5.30 a.m. — At	
NOYANT. NOYON 4 P.M.	At NOYON Brigade Headquarters (G.O.C. only) arrived at Headquarters & I reported that TRAIN was there and complete. — At 4.30 P.M. went with Supply Sections & filled up from Train at Railway (Station). —	
28th. NOYON	Filled up from Rail at NOYON in early morning and then marched, as ordered, to PONTOISE: — where Brigade arrived and billeted the night. —	
29th PONTOISE	At 6 P.M. ordered to march to CARLEPONT. — Halted there and at midnight as-filled from Supply Column. — Remained, as directed, on roadside awaiting orders all night. —	
30th CARLEPONT	AT 7. a.m. ordered to proceed towards COURTOY. — On arrival at ATTICHY received orders to bivouac at	

War Diary

19th Infantry Brigade Train.

Hour	Date	Place	Summary of Events & Information	Remarks & references to appendices
	31st August	COULOISY	COULOISY where arrived about 5 p.m. — Filled from Supply Column about 7 p.m. — Went as ordered, personally, to G.H.Q. at COMPEIGNE to give information re Train personnel to D. of T. — Returned to COULOISY at 12.30 a.m. — COULOISY. Orders to proceed at 6 a.m. to VERBERIE. — On arrival there Counter-orders received for Train to bivouac at SAINTINES.	The Train horses suffered very considerably both from galls and fatigue during this march in great heat. — Only two, however, died from exhaustion. — J. Clifton — Capt. A.S.C. O.C. XIXth Infantry Brigade Train.

19th Infantry Brigade.

T R A I N

19th INFANTRY BRIGADE

SEPTEMBER 1914.

Confidential.

19th Infantry Brigade Train
War Diary

Hour, Date & Place	Summary of Events & Information	Remarks & reference to Appendices
September 1914 1st 5 a.m. SAINTINES - BARON	At 12.5 a.m. Ordered to proceed to BARON via St. VAAST and RARY. - At St. VAAST refilled from roadside dump. - While marching train came under the enemies fire. - 5.30 a.m. arrived BARON roam. - Refilled again, at BARON and took supplies to FRESNOY. - Train ordered to move at 11.30 p.m. from BARON to DAMMARTIN where arrived there 5 a.m.	*2nd line Transport Officer Argyle & Sutherland Highlanders had horse shot under him. JKJ
September 2nd 5 a.m. DAMMARTIN	Filled from Supply Column at 6 p.m. and bivouacked at LONG PERRIER left at 10 p.m. for LAGNY. Snowed all night and arrived at LAGNY at 4.30 a.m.	JKJ
September 3rd 4.30 a.m. LAGNY	and proceeded to BOIS de CHIGNY were remained during the day and refilled from Supply Column in evening. - At JOSSIGNY - Returned and bivouacked for night at BOIS de CHIGNY	JKJ
September 4th BOIS de CHIGNY	Owing to disorganisation of Traffic in Paris Supply Column did not arrive till after Train had started at 11 p.m. to march to BRIE COMTE ROBERT. Arrived at 4 a.m. - At 9 a.m. received ordered to proceed to GRISY where on arrival	JKJ
September 5th BRIE COMTE ROBERT	Train parked for the day and at 3 p.m. filled from Supply Column.	"O" bn "H.Q" Base G.H.Q. Issue of supplies much delayed at railhead owing to disorganisation of traffic in PARIS. JKJ 4.9.14 3 p.m. 3rd A.C. LAGNY

War Diary

Hour Date & Place	Summary of Events & Information	Remarks & references to appendices
September 6th GRISY	At 6.30am ordered to meet train to OZOIR LA FERRIER where re-filled in evening from Supply Column. After refilling marched to VILLENEUVE ST DENIS arrived there 12 midnight	JW.
September 7th VILLENEUVE ST DENIS	9.25am. Baggage section sent to ROMAN VILLIERS as ordered. Supply Section refilled at VILLENEUVE ST DENIS and at 3p.m. proceeded to ROMANVILLIERS and got orders to go on to VILLIERS sur MORIN and await orders there. No further orders being received parked for night there.	JW.
September 8th VILLERS sur MORIN	6am. Ordered to proceed to LA HAUTE MAISON and there informed Brigade was at PIERRE LEVEE. Refilled at PIERRE LEVEE and proceeded at once as ordered to SIGNY-SIGNETS.	JW.
September 9th 2am PIERRE LEVEE	Ordered to take Train back to PIERRE LEVEE and LA GRANDE LOGE FARM at 6.30am ordered to refill there from Supply Column. Arranged and filled at 10.30am and again at 6.20pm. There proceeded to JOUARRIE where arrived at 11.30pm.	JW.
September 10th JOUARRE	At 12.30am ordered to LE GRANDE d LAITET arrived there at 2am. Crossed Pontoon at LAFERTE at 6pm and marched to point 209 (Depot of COCHEREZ). Took supplies to Brigade at CERTIGNY and returned to Point 209 at 1am	JW.

War Diary

Hour Date & Place	Summary of Events & Information	Remarks & references to appendices
September 11th EAST OF COCHEREZ	At 9 a.m. filled from Supply Column at Point 209. At 12-30 p.m. ordered to march to CERFROID and thence to MARIZY ST GENEVIEVE where arrived at 3.a.m.	
September 12th MARIZY ST GENEVIEVE	Baggage section of train left at 12 mid-day with orders to proceed to SEPTMONTES. Supply Settions after re-filling moved off about 2-30 p.m. On leaving MARIZY, train (Supply Sections) came under enemies fire at CHOUY, without casualty. At VILLERS HELON owing to the state of roads and the weather the horses could not be moved further South. No information had been received as to whereabouts of Brigade which had left "P" the direction of SEPTMONTS: at 5 a.m Supply Sections continued march towards SEPTMONTS and orders were received on the march to proceed to BUZANCY where it was notified Brigade had passed the night	
September 13th VILLERS HELON	At 12 noon refilled from Supply Column and at 6 p.m marched the ordered to LE CARRIERE L'EVEQUE.	
September 14th LE CARRIERE L'EVEQUE	Train moved back to SEPTMONTS at 6 a.m. Filled with supplies 3 p.m. and took supplies to VENIZEZ and returned at 7 p.m	
September 15th SEPTMONTS	Still parked at SEPTMONTS. Refilled from Supply Column at 2-30 p.m. At 7 p.m took supplies to VENIZEZ when train refilled	
16	do	
17	do	
18	do	
19	do	
20, 21	do	
22, 23		× On 23rd One extra days rations brought up by supply Column
	{ Brigade Halted at SEPTMONTS & Train Refilled daily. }	

War Diary

Hour, Date, Place	Summary of Events & Information	Remarks & references to Appendices
SEPTMONTS		
September 25: 1914 -	Brigade at Staff SEPTMONTS : Train refilled	9/M
" 26. "	do.	9/M
" 27. "	do.	9/M
" 28. "	do. Captain J. W. Cunningham Acc. arrived at Staff.	9/M.
" 29 "	do. CAPTAIN A. CLIFTON-SHELLEN A.S.C. handed over command of Train to Captain J. W. Cunningham A.S.C. and former left to join Advanced Base Horse Transport Depot. —	J.W.S. A. Clifton-Shellen Capt ASC (late) O.C. 16th Infantry Bgde. Train
SEPTMONTS. Sept. 30 = .	Brigade at SEPTMONTS. Train refilled. 9/M	J.W.Cunningham Capt A.S.C. O.C. 16 Infy Bde. Train.

121/1084

(1st) Confidential.

War Diary
of
O.C. 19th Infantry Brigade Train.

from 1/9/14 to 30/9/14.

Volume II.

19th Brigade.

T R A I N

19th INFANTRY BRIGADE

OCTOBER 1914.

Omg 3/5/6

121/1965

19th Brigade Train

Vol III 1–31.10.14

WAR DIARY or INTELLIGENCE SUMMARY.

(Erase heading not required.)

Army Form C. 2118.

Instructions regarding War Diaries and Intelligence Summaries are contained in F.S. Regs., Part II. and the Staff Manual respectively. Title pages will be prepared in manuscript.

Hour, Date, Place	Summary of Events and Information	Remarks and references to Appendices
6.45pm 1/10/14. SEPTMONTS	Brigade at SEPTMONTS. Train refilled	OST
8pm 2/10/14 SEPTMONTS	" " "	OST
8pm 3/10/14 do	" Railhead moved to OULCHY BRENY. Train refilled OST	
8pm 4/10/14 do	" Train refilled	OST
8pm 5/10/14 do	" "	OST
1am 6/10/14 ST.REMY.	Arrived ST. REMY at 8.10 p.m. Train refilled before leaving.	OST
11.45pm 7/10/14 VEZ	Arrived ST.REMY at 1.30 a.m. Train refilled.	OST
	Left REMY 2.8pm marched via VILLERS-COTTERETS arrived 4 a.m. Train refilled	OST
8.10.14 PONT MAXENCE	Left 2.30pm arrived here 5.30 p.m. Train did not refill	OST
9.10.14 ESTREES.ST.DENIS	Left MAXENCE 7.30am arrived ESTREES. 9.30am. Entrained at midnight & left 2.45am. 9.2 Brns. 2 days supplies from Railway Supply Column. Supp Coln off loaded to VI. Division arrived ARQUES 5pm. Train refilled (ABBEVILLE) Opn
10.10.14 WATTEN	Travelled via BOULOGNE and CALAIS. arrived 5pm. Train refilled 9.30pm. per ST.OMER. 3.30pm arrived ARQUES 5pm. Train refilled	OST
11.10.14 ST.OMER	Arrived about 12.5 am. Left 7.30am and arrived ARQUES 9am. Transported March'd again 5pm arrived ARENNES & BORE Supply column 5pm	OST
12.10.14 BORRE	Marched at 6.50 am. via EBBLINGHEM; arrived 9pm. Train refilled 3 a.m. 13th Brigade joined. OST
10pm. 13.10.14. Think N.M. BORRE	Marched to this point at 7 am. + parked. Brigade at ROUGE CROIX. Train refilled 8pm Brigade disengaged OST
14.x.14 BAILLEUL	Arrived 5pm Bde in outposts did not fill carts over till 11pm. Train refilled 2 am. Billeted.	OST
15. x. 14 do	Halted all day here. nothing doing	OST
16.x.14 VLAMERTINGHE	Marched 9 am to STEENWERCK and thence to VLAMERTINGHE in Belgium arriving 8pm. Columns arrived midnight.	OST
17.x.14	From this date no longer belong to VI Division. Halted all day in billets.	OST

WAR DIARY.

18.X.14	VLAMERTINGHE	Halted all day. Train refilled. 2nd Ech.
19.X.14	do.	do.
20.X.14	LAVENTIE	Handed for LAVENTIE via STEENWERCK at 2 p.m. Refilled STEENWERCK. 2nd Ech.
21.X.14	SAILLY sur LYS	Arrived 5.30 a.m; delayed owing to part of transport having taken wrong road in the darkness. 2nd Ech.
22.X.14	do	Arrived 1 p.m. Brigade at FROMELLES. Train refilled. 2nd Ech
23.X.14	do	Brigade at CROIX BLANCHE " " 2nd Ech
24.X.14	do	LA BOUTILLERIE " " 2nd Ech
25.X.14	do	" do " " 2nd Ech
26.X.14	do	" do " " 2nd Ech
27.X.14	do	" Railhead moved to ST. VENANT from MERVILLE 2nd Ech
28.X.14	do	Requisitioned 12 teams for 1st Middlesex Regiment symbol 20 2nd Ech
29.X.14	do	do 2nd Ech
30.X.14	do	do 2nd Ech
31.X.14	do	do 2nd Ech

H. Henning Leem
Capt. etc.
O.C. 19. "Coy" B.dE Train.

19th Brigade

T R A I N

19th INFANTRY BRIGADE

NOVEMBER 1914.

121/2625

19th Brigade. Train.

Vol IV. 1—30.11.14

War Diary for NOVEMBER

19th Infantry Brigade Train

Hour	Date	Place	Summary of Events & Information	Remarks & references to appendices
	1.11.14	SAILLY sur LYS (in Trokes near Brigade Bat.)	CROIX BLANCHE Railhead ST VENANT. Train refilled SAILLY.	Bat.
	2.11.14	do	do do do	Bat.
	3.11.14	do	do do	Bat.
	4.11.14	do	do do	Bat.
	5.11.14	do	Requisitioned and paid for 1 horse cart and harness of CÉSAR TANCRÉ of DOULIEU at ESTAIRES Bat.	
	6.11.14	do	Nothing to record, no move. Bat.	
	7.11.14	do	Bought 4 horses, harness and carts for blankets, 3 for Field Ambulance and one for Bde Hd Qrs from (1) VEUVE MARTIN at VERGUIN	
			(2) The horse from Chr HAELEWYN at MERVILLE (iii) one cart and harness from E. DORIEZ at VERGUIN (iv) one cart and harness from	
	8.11.14	do	Francl GUEFROY at VERGUIN (V) who hires 1 cart + harness from M. PRESSE at VERGUIN, all by order of G.O.C. Bat.	
	9.11.14	do	Nothing to record. 3 drivers with carts detached to Field Ambulance Bat.	
	10.11.14	do	Nothing to record. Bat. and detailed for transport duty and	
	11.11.14	do	2/Lt. M.M. PAKENHAM joined for duty from home, 19 remounts arrived to Brigade Bat.	
	12.11.14	do	Nothing to record. Remounts distributed to units. A/Lt. Pakenham arrived reported by letter to D.J.T. Bat.	
	13.11.14	do	Neill Brodie Hurmy ordered by G.O.C. to leave him to take charge of 2 line transport while Brian is temp. compelled with order after saying and ...	(Think it necessary for him to leave the Train) Bat.
	14.11.14	do	Bde retired in trenches by 7 Div. let at night	
	15.11.14	do	Received two horses from No 6 Mobile Section, 1 riding, 1 draught. Bat.	
	16.11.14	do		
	17.11.14	NIEPPE (nr LES TROIS TILLEULS)	Brigade moved to new position near HOUPLINES. Railhead MERVILLE. I have handed to mobile section and refilling point at LES TROIS TILLEULS. 1 drive Tpt in ARMENTIERES Bat.
	18.11.14	do	Nothing to record Bat.	
	19.11.14	do	5th Scottish Rifles attached to the Brigade. Bat.	
	20.11.14	do	Inspected transport of 5th Scottish Rifles, they have heavy 4 wheeled wagons of SAA and 1st line carts — reported unavailability to G.O.C.	
	21.11.14	do	On duty the Wear of their regiment returned to Nº 4 Mobile Section. Bat.	
			Arrived per Bde H.Q. Nº 2 Known are 4 horsed H.D. horses Nº 1 H.Q. 1st Post wagons. Ft. A.S. Highlanders 5 drivers 8 L.D. 2 H.D. 4 SAA carts, 1 T. wagon on	
	22.11.14	do	Nothing to record. Bat.	Ft. Ar Delivery 5 drivers 1 OLD. 4 SAH carts. Ft. Train HQ 4 Sgt Singart 2 MCO 8 drivers 4 PLs. Railhead STEENWERCK Bat.
	23.11.14	do	5 L.D. returned from A. + S.H. + transferred to 5th Scottish Rifles inct 4 SAA carb. SHDb Nº 6 Mobile Section. 5 L.D. bs 1 kg 6 Div Train	
			Capt Omniolles went to England on 10 days leave	

War Diary for NOVEMBER.
19th Infantry Brigade Train

Hour	Date	Place	Summary of Events & Information	Remarks & references to appendices
	24.11.14	Nr NIEPPE (LRS TROIS TILLEULS)	Inspected 19th Rfts Fd Ambulance & reported to 6th Divn. Pointed out large discrepancy between what should be in the ration stacks & what there was. 1 ZDA Kin Ambulance D.z.b.	
	25.11.14	d.c.	On tour, reported last night of A & B Hyl dn & trans Tpt. D.z.b.	
	26.11.14	do.	On tour commission short of 1 Veby Officer. Need Ypt. 3 carcass-beam bad. Bread good weight. Ipt.	
	27.11.14	do.	Recommended Sgt Major 2 & Rakman for promotion to 2nd Rt. to Dy.T G.H.E. Supply Officer can be PARIS trenzfain. Ipt.	
	28.11.14	do.	1 H.D. Horse of Coy H.Q. died of pneumonia. Pt. Tafner, A. MT driver returned to Base MT depot. Statement of Field Hstp. Y.J.an. 1940. B.z.b. Bread (Fresh) again short weight & on exception in 30%. D.z.b. Nothing to record. D.z.b.	
	29.11.14	do.	4 wagons, 6 horses H.D. 8 oats and lime ham low 2 trust collars & 5 battle Rifles fusil on mit per Base Horse Transport depot. HAVRE. Ordered 20 trust tons of coal at BAILLEUL to be delivered at STEENWERCK railway station. D.z.b.	
	30.11.14	do.		

H.Manning Lenn
Captain, A.S.C.
O.C. 19th Infantry Brigade Train

19th Brigade.

T R A I N

19th INFANTRY BRIGADE

DECEMBER 1914.

121/3976

19th Brigade Train.

Vol V. 1 — 31.12.14

War Diary — DECEMBER 1914
19th Infantry Brigade Train

Hour, Date, Place	Summary of Events & Information	Remarks & reference to appendices

LES TROIS TILLEULS
(Nr PONT DE NIEPPE)

1st Dec. 1914 — Brig. Genl. R.W. Thom. visited the Trait. 3 L.D. horses received from 1 Coy. 6th Bn. Train. Posted to Brig. T. Nov. 11. A.G. 3rd Echelon Base. Received notification from Adjt. 6th Bn. Train that I am to return home as 6th Bn. adm.

2nd Dec. 1914 do — Visit of H.M. King to L'EPINETTE — 2 officers & 8 N.C.O.'s & men between Train, Supply Col. + R.E. Amn. Col. attended. B.S.C.

3rd Dec. 1914 do — Inspection 1st Line Tpt. horses by O.C. 6th Divn. 1 H.D. of R.W.F. train wagon died yesterday of B.S.C.

4th Dec. 1914 do — 2 draught horses recd. from VI Divn. Train.

5th Dec. 1914 do — Nothing to record. Complaints of shortage of head rope to it crumbling — about 25% shortage. B.S.C. Handed over command of Train to Capt. J. Blount. Demand the proceed to returning to England on 6th Dec.
{One L.D. horse (Hindenburg) died yesterday — advice/rec. B.S.C.}

6-12-14 — Capt. E.W. Cunningham proceeded to England with instructions to report at War Office. Capt. L.A.K. Carter, O/C. 1st Line Tpt. B.S.C. Supply Column, proceeded to England on 10 days leave. Lt. J. Tyler is acting for him. Lt. W.B. Flook, 1/c Ammunition Column also proceeded to England on 10 days leave; Lt. K.A. Brooke-Taylor is answering for him. New Ford lorry of Liddells-Army Car broke his moorings; this was repaired in column workshop and car returned to evening. Lens mud guards were also fitted. B.S.C.

7-12-14 — 3.2.5 Reinforcements arrived today. Went to railhead & got extra rations for Rem. 1 Riding horse rec. for 6th Bn.

8-12-14 — In conjunction with Lt. Irvine A.V.C. his picked horses off 1st Line Transport, with particular reference to the shoeing. Satisfactory on the whole with the exception of the 2/A.O.S. A/ Aberdeen, where the shoeing has been greatly neglected. 1 Train horse developed Strangles. B.S.C.

9-12-14 — 290 Reinforcements arrived today. Went to railhead & got extra rations for Rem. 3 Riding horses rec. for 6th Bn. B.V.O.

10-12-14 — 1 L.D. horse of Field Ambulance Shot today. B.V.O. for debility. 1 Train horse developed Strangles. Refilled under tent at Train Billet & machinery. Also had quantity of Chaff Cut B.S.C.

War Diary

Date	Place	Summary of events & information	Remarks references to appendices
11-12-14	LES 3 TILLEULS, FRANCE.	Went to B.H.Q. at ST. OMER & got new Humber motor car to replace Rolls Royce car, raced to Paris on 27th ult. 2 men R.D. horses of the Train decorated Rigaum. /F25	
12-12-14		Interview with S.S.O. 6th Div. at CROIX DU BAC re supplies. /F25	
13-12-14		100 reinforcements arrived. 1 Riding horse died (rupture) of L.D. horses of 19th Field ambulance shot by V.O. for shocked mange. Sent 3 L.D. horses to 1/Scottish Rifles to complete establishment. /F25	
14-12-14		Heavy shelling of ARMENTIERES took place tonight shortest range of Rungrout the night Regt. at war. Transport had to quit their billets next to PONT DE NIEPPE. No casualties; only damage done to the transport lines was her rabbit split killed. /F25	
15-12-14		Started system of (sending units) independently to railhead for coal & coke. Began higher coal convoys. The baggage wagons of the Regt. went under the command of 2/Lt. Packenham to STEENWERCK and drew coal stock direct to the Regtl. billets. A 10 ton truck can be cleared in a day and 1 continue no convoy daily till all requirements for a week are sent up. Requirements for this week 30 tons /F25	
16-12-14		Coal convoy under 2/Lt Edgell proceeded the same as yesterday. Inspected 1st Line horses with Lt. Irwin A.V.C. Great improvement noticed, especially as regards 2/Brgd & 3rd Richard & 4th Pleaden. /F25	
17-12-14		Received instructions that Brigade has to arrange for local repair of boots & necessary material for repair could be for Regt. Lt. Col. H. Bevis, Commanding 6th Aux Train, inspected his Train, billets, horses etc. & expressed himself well satisfied with what he saw. /F25	
18-12-14		Attack by Allies along whole line ARMENTIERES – ARRAS. Some trenches taken retained /F25	

War Diary

Hour Date Place	Summary of events and information	Remarks & references to Appendices
LES 3 TILLEULS, FRANCE 19-12-14	Railway Supply Train late again, with the result that Column did not arrive till about H.P.D. It was dark before refilling could commence. This refilling in the dark bad weather is very unsatisfactory and after consultation with the G.O.C. have decided to adopt same system as H. of 1st Division. Rats, The Column fills at Railhead so soon as it is filled: loaded overnight comes up to Refilling Point first thing the following morning. Then goes to Railhead to reload for the following day. JPS.	
20-12-14	No refilling took place today as new system is to be adopted tomorrow. Coal convoy from STEENWERCK under Lt Packenham. JPS.	
21-12-14	Started new system of refilling. Column arrived at 6.30 a.m. & dumped & then refilling into Supply began proceeded. Daylight refilling is much preferable. Hope to arrive at same time i.e. 1.30 p.m. JPS.	
22-12-14	Lt. J. Tyler, Supply Column & C.S.M. Fowle proceeded today to England on 10 days leave of absence. Went to B. H.Q. today to interview D. of T. regarding certain Transport question.	
23-12-14	Major C. Furneaux acting O.C. 6th Div. Train, made an inspection this afternoon of 1st Line Transport. I held an inspection in conjunction with Lt Irwin this morning.	
24-12-14	Returned 2nd Motor-Car, the Siddeley-Deasy, with Pte Hallen to Army Troops Supply Coln. at B.H.Q. An instruction received from D. of T. Inspected NIEPPE HALTE with view to Refilling from Railway Train stand. As there is no siding & refilling is practically impossible Rue Wants from BAILLEUL ordered 40 tons of coal to be sent. Plum puddings were issued holes to the units JPS.	
25-12-14	Distributed Pres Majesties' Xmas cards & winners many gifts to the men. JPS.	

War Diary

Hour, Date, Place	Summary of events & information	Remarks & references to Appendices
LES 3 TILLEULS FRANCE 26-12-14	Cote Supply at ARMENTIERES for works as marked. Attended conference of Supply Officers at Head Quarters of 3rd Corps. Lt. R.A. Brooke-Murray returned to the Train for duty as Transport Sub-Lieut. after being Bde Transport Officer.	
27-12-14	Canvased Regts. for lists of names of those receiving Princess Mary's Gift. Great difficulty experienced in obtaining them as it is difficult for Regts. in the trenches to make Returns wh. has	purchased which are
28-12-14	Paid Regts. for Mess Carts and Harness which they had previously now being taken over by the Govt. &S.	Horses are old Monarchs wn
29-12-14	Wheels of Blanket cart of 2 R. Welch Fusiliers collapsed. Dies are old not arranged to have 2 new ones made locally. &S. Lt. Col. Robertson, The Cameronians (acting O.C. 19th Inf. Bde) inspected the Train this morning. He saw Refilling in progress & afterwards inspected the Billets. Expressed himself as very well satisfied. Coal ordered to be at NIEPPE today did not arrive. &S.	
30-12-14		
31-12-14	40 tons of coal arrived at NIEPPE HALTE this afternoon. Lt. R.A. Brooke-Murray left the Train proceeded by empty Railway Supply Train from STEENWERCK to Advanced Horse Transport Depot, to take up the duties of noting together Res.	

Edward Armitelli Capt.
O.C. 19th Inf. Bde Train.

121/4261

19th Brigade Train

Vol VI. 1 - 31.1.16

War Diary January 1914
XIX H.Q. B[atta]lion Train

Hour	Date	Place	Summary of events + information	Remarks + reference to Appendices
	1-1-15	LES 3 TILLEULS FRANCE	Nothing to record	yes
	2-1-15		B[attalio]n relieved 16th B[attalio]n in trenches in front of BOIS GRENIER night. Sent wagon to Railhead to draw coke as was unable to get coke. Was heal [unreadable] warmer. Only able to get about 1 cwt. & this per Regt. Attended conference of S[upply] Officers at H[ea]d Q[uar]rs 3rd Corps.	yes
	3-1-15		There was no coke at Railhead today. So issued a paper load I had in reserve & had to make up with sacks of Char coal. Grew cool from Railhead from 6th Division, to make up to get it turn in future. 2 H.D. 2 L.D. & 4 Rifling horse arrived from 6th Div. Were 1 H.R.s from Capt H.T. Ribot of 2 R Welch Fusiliers for the relief of Field General Court Martial held today at billets of 2 R.W.F. Fusiliers for the relief	yes
	4-1-15		Prov: C[or]pl. Shreghnam who was charged with being drunk on New Years Day. Temp[orarily] 2 Lt. I.C.V. Smith joined today in relief of Lt. K.A. Brooks-Murray.	yes
	5-1-15		Found no regristic[?] in some stacks of straw at CHAPELLE D'ARMENTIERES, which I found were being threshed today. 1 water cart arrived him at [unreadable] water for the 1st time.	yes
	6-1-15		Train: There were also deserted him at which arrived for the 1st time. Col[one]l S. L[ieu]t. West + Sgt. Fosken admitted to A.P. - defective teeth. Nothing to record.	yes
	7-1-15		Promulgated Proceedings of F.G.C.M. on Prov: Cpl. Shreghnam, who was sentenced to be reduced to the rank & to be fined #1. One month Field Punishment No 1 also Awarded were remitted by G.O.C. 19th Inf. B[riga]de.	yes

War Diary January 1915

XIX Bde: B Cy: Train

Hour	Date	Place	Summary of Events & information	Remarks & References to appendices
		LES BILLEULS	Requisitioned Field Forge on temp'y loan for use of our Shoeing Smiths amongst the horses, which are necessary to be shod. JAS	Field Maintenance
	7-1-15			
	8-1-15		Nothing to record. JAS	
	9-1-15		Attended conference of Supply Officers at H.Q. 9th & 3rd Cav. Supported issue of Curry Powder to troops in lieu of mustard once a week. Inspected 1st line horses. JAS	
	10-1-15		Exchanged old Cars, which have now become obsolete for new one. Temp'y 2nd Lt. B.V.H. McLellan joined today in relief of Lt. K.A. Brooke-Murray. 2nd Lt. J.R. Edgell proceeded to England tonight on 8 days leave. Brigadier Gen: Boyce & D.D.S.T., paid a surprise visit & inspected the Train billets and horses as were in. Dmr. Bailey arrived with 2nd Lt. McLellan on his account. Dvr. C. Tromp admitted to R. JAS	
	11-1-15		Having discovered that nearly all the N.C.Os & men of the company had not been inoculated against Typhoid Fever; that the rest majority were unwilling to be done. I addressed the men on parade and endeavoured to point out to them the advantages of such inoculation. One of the civilian wagons with small fire wheels, in charge of the 5th Scottish Rifles, got stuck in the mud whilst loaded with coal at STEENWERCK & the front broken of fore-carriage broke. This was temporarily repaired and the wagon brought back to billet for further repairs. 2nd Lt. McLellan's horse slipped up with him & broke his ankle, necessitating a rest for several days. He had it attended to by the M.O. JAS	
	12-1-15		Temp'y Lt. A. Buckmaster arrived for duty as Requisitioning Officer. S.M. Boatman proceeded tonight on 8 days leave to England. A ration of 1 oz of tea loaf for each man in the trenches was made issued today for the first time. 100 lbs. of marmalade received & distributed amongst the different units. This is the first lot received for many weeks. About 30 N.C.Os & men had 1st dose of inoculation this morning, I relieved men of all duties for rest of day whilst so for however. A few O.R.s were badly affected. One H.D. horse to horse shoeing section defective front. JAS	
	13-1-15			

War Diary

Hour, Date, Place	Summary of events and information	Remarks & references to appendices
LES 3 TILLEULS FRANCE. 14-1-15	250 lb. mandleds received & distributed to 1st Line Column, 2 R.W. Fusiliers, The Cameronians. Pte Barritt transferred to 6th Div: Train in Hd Qr. Office. There were still 9 men who objected being inoculated, so of 6th Div. Train in order that men might hear the views of Lt. Col. H. Davies. Lecture had the desired effect for this all subsequently expressed themselves willing to be inoculated.	horses of Ammunition Provein for clerks, one clerk marched down to HQ on the subject. His Jas.
15-1-15	Inspected 1st line horses of 5th Scottish Rifles, 1st Middlesex, 2nd A.S.C. H.T. Received notification that Capt. J. Blount-Dinniddie has been appointed Temp: Major to date Nov: 30th 1914. Jas.	1st 19th Field Ambulance.
16-1-15	Attended Supply Officers' Conference at 3rd Corps HQ. It was decided to recommend that issue of dried fruits in lieu of jam be discontinued on Mon. as not popular with men. About another 30 men had their 1st dose of anti-typhoid inoculation.	Not issue of dried 1st Remembrance and Jas
17-1-15	Inspection of N.C.Os & men of Ps Companies in marching order by Lt. Col. H. Davies, O.C. 6th Div. Train. Jas	
18-1-15	Lt. J.A. Edgell returned from leave & Temp: Lt. J.C.V. Smith returned to 6th Div: Train for duty. 1 H.D. horse to mobile section – laminitis.	Jas
19-1-15	Gift of tinned Salmon received from British Columbia distributed amongst troops. Very good indeed appreciated.	Jas
20-1-15	T. Major J. Blount Dinniddie was President of Court of Enquiry at Middlesex Billet to investigate & report upon circumstances under which a fire took place in Nat Regt's Billet on night of 29-30th Dec. '14. S.M. Bottom returned from leave. Dvr. Cocklin, Fingrom, Fletcher (motors) Branes from 19th F.A. amblen & to 19th F.A.	
21-1-15	Inspected horses of 1st Line in conjunction with A.D.V.S. 6th Division. Field Ambulance found it not to be worth repair. Complaint received from O.C. 2/A.N. Hrs as to Canvas Stack of Bread. Biscuit issued in lieu to make up deficiency.	Inspected blanket cart of 19th F.A. Jas
22-1-15	Refilling Point changed to ERQUINGHEM at road junction of RUE DES ACQUETS. De cente vehicles from each Regt. came rather than direct as this place is close to all 1st Line Billets. This	

War Diary

Unit, Date, Place	Summary of events and information	Remarks & references to Appendices
LES 3 TILLEULS FRANCE 22-1-15	Ration is now convenient for all concerned. The Supply wagons are now released for drawing coal and coke from Railhead daily; also for straw + charcoal; the Baggage wagons are often used by Regts. When in billets and are also used for conveying Ordnance Stores. Orders received that S.m. Postman placed on probation for 1st Cl: S.S.M., + C.S.M. Forde + C.Q.M.S. Rolfe on probation for S.S.M. One civilian pattern wagon of the 52nd Northd. Rifles, drawing coal at STEENWERCK, got stuck in the mud + the pole was broken.	Jps
23-1-15	S.M. Postman gazetted Q: ms to 2nd Bn K.R.R. Attended Supply Officers conference at H.Q. 3rd Corps. All C².s. of cokes charcoal rations increased to 2 lb. per man in the trenches.	Jps
24-1-15	3½ tons Charcoal received sure kept issued out to units in trenches at rate of 2 lb per man	Jps
25-1-15	2Lt. White-Jones arrived from Paris H.T. Depot; Sgt. Adamson of 19th Fusiliers from 19th Field Ambulance joined. R.O. Returned to 1st Line R. of H.Q., M. Rolle to A.P.	Jps
26-1-15	Inspected horses of 19th Field Ambulance. They are now free of mange. The 2nd 4 hands of N.C.O. men had 2½ inoculation dose. Pte afternoon G.O.C. Ferguson + F.Rollers to 19th Field Ambulance	Jps
27-1-15	R.O. checked stocks of entrenched stores behind lines of 19th Inf. Bd.	Jps
28-1-15	S.M. M. Peterborough proceeded to hospt on 8 days leave to England. Cpl. Robinson + L/Cpl. Ferguson from 19th Field ambulance. Inspected horses of 5th Scottish Rifles, Middlesex, + 2/H.L. Highrs. Had water tanks at Billet refilled.	Jps
29-1-15	Inspected horses of the Cameronians, R. Welsh Fusiliers, Ammunition column. Sgt. Peebles arrived from 6th Divn. on probation as C.S.M. L.Cpl. Rolfe to 6th Division Train on probation as S.S.M.	Jps
30-1-15	Attended conference of Supply Officers at H.Q. 3rd Corps. Increase of Bag. w.12 Lb. per horse ordered for	Jps
31-1-15	Railhead changed to STRAZEELE, + consequent delay in arrival of Mails + Papers. Q: m/ s/Mm L. t W. G. Postman proceeded to England tonight with orders to report to D. of S. at War Office. Sgt. Powell went on 5 days leave to England	Jps

J Belmont Maj'r
D.C. 19th M.B. Batt n rain
O.C. 19th M.B. Batt n rain

19th Brigade Train
Vol VII 1 — 28.2.15

WAR DIARY XIX Ind. Bde Train

INTELLIGENCE SUMMARY

Army Form C. 2118.

(Erase heading not required.)

Hour, Date, Place	Summary of Events and Information	Remarks and references to Appendices
LES 3 TILLEULS, FRANCE. 1-2-15	209 Reinforcements arrived for the Bde. Railhead changed back to STEENWERCK. Received 6 British trucks from A.O.D. Pte Mitchell admitted to H.H. & sent to Base.	Jns
2-2-15	Complaint received from 2/R.W. Fusiliers that weight of Bx. cos. is 10 to 15 lbs. less than recorded on the Box.	Jns Aco 2
3-2-15	6 cases of Bacon weighed this morning, 1 found to be exact weight as recorded on Box, & 3 weighed one lb. more. Pte Bedward reported from 1st Line, 13th Fd Amb. Pte Wheelhouse admitted to Hospital from Base. Inspected horses of 1st Line, received 15th Scottish Rifles Rv.O. Also went & inspected all horses in order to find out those in foal, no Regt are to be returned to the Base. Received notification that Sergt L.A.K. Carter is to take over command of No. 2 Indian Ammunition Park. 2nd Lt H.G. Dankery will take over command of the Supply Colm from him.	Jns
4-2-15	Weighed 6 cases of Bacon, stood all to be as recorded on Box. Inspected horses of 1st Line, 5th Scottish Rifles. No coke arrived at Railhead today, but have received sufficient from a reserve to take Lt Mitchell both cases off 3 wagons to STEENWERCK, got 13 tons of coal. Lt. G. Richardson Qr Mr right for 8 days leave in England.	Jns

Army Form C. 2118.

WAR DIARY
or
INTELLIGENCE SUMMARY. XIX hf. B. d. Train

(Erase heading not required.)

Instructions regarding War Diaries and Intelligence Summaries are contained in F.S. Regs., Part II and the Staff Manual respectively. Title pages will be prepared in manuscript.

Hour, Date, Place	Summary of Events and Information	Remarks and references to Appendices
LES TILLEULS, FRANCE 5-2-15	6 more Boxes of Bacon weighed today & found to be as recorded on the GRC. 2/L. M. Pakenham should have returned from leave last night but failed to do so. Fact reported to Adjt. 6th Divl. Train. Sent a horse to replace mare (in foal) in the Post Office Cart. No coke arrived at Railhead, had not sufficient in reserve store for requirements. Sgt. Bevill returned from leave & Sgt. Briston left for 5 days leave in England. Sgt. HQ Derby arrived & took over command of Supply Column.	fbs
6-2-15	Began I.A.C. Carter left today for No 2 Indian Ammunition Park. No Supply Train arrived for No. 6 B.S. today. Supplies had to be drawn from Reserve Stock at Railhead. In consequence Park was no need of a fresh meat, with preserve & bacon no rest having to be made up by issue of butter. Attended conference of SHRB officers at 3rd Corps HQ. Wished had been found might again create. Informed unit train scales would be very reduced now & have been adjusted. 7/14989 Sgt. Gale, T joined from 6th Divl. Train.	fbs
7-2-15	D. Honeybourne admitted to H. Inspected horses of 18 co. HQ.1 several receiving shoeing balls; obtained new issues. 2/Lt. M. Pakenham returned from leave tonight. He had been sick had had medical official certificate to the effect that he had influenza over so ill to read on the day he should have come down. It also reported to the War Office.	fbs

Army Form C. 2118.

WAR DIARY
or
INTELLIGENCE SUMMARY. XIX Hy. Bty. T.R.sm.
(Erase heading not required.)

Instructions regarding War Diaries and Intelligence Summaries are contained in F.S. Regs., Part II. and the Staff Manual respectively. Title pages will be prepared in manuscript.

Hour, Date, Place	Summary of Events and Information	Remarks and references to Appendices
LES 3 TILLEULS, FRANCE 9-2-15	Had football for an hour with Spare men. Considering that all are extra Reservists or specially enlisted divisors the result was extremely satisfactory. Dr. Honeybourne transferred to Base H. 2 N.C.O.s in fuel sent to hostile section.	yes
10-2-15	Interviewed manager of ARMENTIÈRES gasworks re. having to cool works taken from gaswork. He has not got all the required quantities but he went to Lt. Perrin for cost. 1,209 per recto. He preferred market office to 62 Picotain before paying. 509	
	The Company went to performance of the Follies at ARMENTIÈRES. Major Coc went to Field Ambulance for duty. Sgt. Bristow returned from leave, & Dvr. Wiles proceeded on leave to England for 5 days.	yes
11-2-15	Inspected horses of 1st line of Amb. Hdm. 1/Middlesex Regt. ammunition column C.S.M. Forde, B.Q.M.S. 6th. Sect. Train on probation.	yes
	A.J.S.M.	
12-2-15	Had water tanks filled again today, as the Engineer who runs the engine is going off in 2 days time to join the French army. Inspected 1st line horses of the Cameronians, 2/R.W.F., & 5th. Scottish Rifles, & Field Ambulance. Lt. A. Renshaw returned from leave.	yes

Army Form C. 2118.

WAR DIARY
or
INTELLIGENCE SUMMARY. XIX h.f: B.t. Train

(Erase heading not required.)

Instructions regarding War Diaries and Intelligence Summaries are contained in F.S. Regs., Part II. and the Staff Manual respectively. Title pages will be prepared in manuscript.

Hour, Date, Place	Summary of Events and Information	Remarks and references to Appendices
LES 3 TILLEULS, FRANCE 13-2-15	There was no coke at Railhead & had to send to CROIX DU BAC for it. Lt. Akenhein took convoy to STEENWERCK to draw coal. One of M.T. wagons got stuck in the deep mud alongside the tracks & one of the poles was broken. The wagon was eventually got out by means of a spare pole. Attended conference of Supply officers at Corps H.Q. Capt. Woodford, Veterinary proceeded to billets with coal wagon, was struck by a stray rifle bullet. Slightly wounded at back of head. His horse received a bullet in buttock, & was later removed to Mobile Veterinary Section. Capt. Woodford was taken to H.P. J. S. M. Newsted, E. priced from 3 Co: 6th Div: Train taken to H.P.	
14-2-15	Lt. Richard replaced Dr. Cre. at Field ambulance. Lt. M. Aluden admitted to H.P. Lt. Pendroton schedched all M. Shans, Mules and rechecked along the road Le Cron—Bailof—Bois Grenier—La Guernerie	pos pos
15-2-15	Settled M. Calhan's claim for shaws taken by units of Inv. 13th Whitstab. HOUPLINES. Dr. G. H. Smith proceeded to Ryland Knightsfor S. clergs leave. Mr. R. Wiles returned from leave. Lt. H. Pohn admitted to H.P. 3 L.O. horses received from 2 Co: 6 Brit. Train to complete establishment 1 M.T. horse sent to Mobile Section.	pos
16-2-15	D.D.O.R. II Army inspected all horses of M. Train, including blanket cart horses, harness, with 12 Div.	pos

WAR DIARY
or
INTELLIGENCE SUMMARY. XIX H.Q. 13th 7th Div.

Army Form C. 2118.

(Erase heading not required.)

Hour, Date, Place	Summary of Events and Information	Remarks and references to Appendices
LES 3 TILLEULS, FRANCE 17-2-15	Inspected horses of 4th Div. Am. Middlesex Regt., Camerons & R.W.F. The Canadian Division arrived today, one Brigade being attached to the 6th Division, the 4th B.G. of which is attached to this B.G. Arrangements for supply of fuel, straw & fresh vegetables are to be made by me, the rest of the supplies being arranged for by men or officers from T. Maher to Field Ambulance	
18-2-15	Two shells burst just over 6th Division Refilling Point about 9.30 a.m. — Not far from our refilling point. 1 horse killed & 2 were wounded. Inspected horses of M.C.S. H.Q. & field Ambulance. 6th Division Farriers commenced rein adjustments in the 19th Field Ambulance billet this afternoon. There are to be 2 performances daily — Sundays excepted — at 3 p.m. & at 6 p.m. Received letter from D. of T. notifying that a certain number of men N.C.O.s would shortly be required to proceed to England to form new formations stating that I had to nominate men from the ranks to take their place.	⟨initials⟩
19-2-15	Inspected horses of 1st Scottish Rifles. Had football for an hour in morning.	⟨initials⟩
20-2-15	Attended conference of supply officers at 3rd Corps H.Q. asked for increase of 5 oz bread ration taken for 1st Div. Daily, news of weather frozen	⟨initials⟩

WAR DIARY
or
INTELLIGENCE SUMMARY. XIX Inf: B⁴ Train

Army Form C. 2118.

(Erase heading not required.)

Instructions regarding War Diaries and Intelligence Summaries are contained in F.S. Regs., Part II. and the Staff Manual respectively. Title pages will be prepared in manuscript.

Hour, Date, Place	Summary of Events and Information	Remarks and references to Appendices
3 TILLEULS, FRANCE 20-2-15	Meat title matter. 12 gift boxes of sweets received from S.R. Cranford, Australia, for general distribution amongst the troops. Sgt. Gould, Lat. of this Train, is mentioned in despatches for good work done in the months of August & September 1914. The list of names "In time" was received today. Capt. (Temp. Major) B.W. Cunningham has also mentioned.	Mjr.
21-2-15	Rev. W. Webb Peploe, C. of E., held a service in the Train billets at 3 p.m. This service was very well attended, though attendance at it was purely voluntary. D.D. Falkner arrived from ROUEN.	Mjr.
22-2-15	Purchased 61 bank trunks for use in the Brigade as A.O.D. notifies that same are not available at the Base & request local purchase to be made as far as possible. 4th Canadian Bgft. again today.	Mjr.
23-2-15	6th Division Refilling Point changed to ARMENTIÈRES. 16th Canadian Bn. Advance party arrived today. The 13th marching to tomorrow. Sgt. Parsgood discovered a dead body of a gunner in the river LYS this morning & reported to Field Ambulance, who had body removed.	Mjr.
24-2-15.	Brig. Gen. Hon. F. Gordon C.B., D.S.O., Comdg. 19th Inf. Bde inspected the Train this afternoon at L'EPINETTE × roads. He saw no wagons marked	Mjr.

WAR DIARY

or

~~INTELLIGENCE SUMMARY.~~ XIX hf. R.d. Train

(Erase heading not required.)

Army Form C. 2118.

Instructions regarding War Diaries and Intelligence Summaries are contained in F.S. Regs., Part II. and the Staff Manual respectively. Title pages will be prepared in manuscript.

Hour, Date, Place	Summary of Events and Information	Remarks and references to Appendices
LES 3 TILLEULS, FRANCE 24-2-15	had him recknowed himself on well satisfied with all the men.	fras.
25-2-15	Dvr Wheeler R.P. Smith & Dvr Phillips, D'gns[?] Gilkes, Bevan, Miller joined from BASE to complete establishment. A/Sgt Cahill, Dvrs Wales, Bennett, & Clark joined from Field Ambulance. A/Sgt Adamson & Dvrs Wilson, Patterson, & Green to Field Ambulance in their place. Saddlr Sgt Ellis & Dvr Cade proceeded this afternoon to ENGLAND for 5 days leave.	fras
26-2-15	Inspected all 1st line horses this morning. & afternoon had foot drill & manual exercise from him. Arranged to requisition potatoes from farm of M. DUMORTIER at BOIS GRENIER, as he wishes to get rid of them. Wrote to Reapr Ham? I can get men for in ARMENTIÈRES i.e. 6f. 100k. Enlisted of 8.50 & 9 f. 100k. began too late after dark to get men got rid of? Filles tonight. fras	fras.
27-2-15	Attended conference of supply officer at 3rd Corps H.Q. asked for increase of coffee rec'd weekly to 400 lbs from 250 lbs, which has previously been coming up. Got 100k of potatoes from BOIS GRENIER tonight.	fras
28-2-15	Saw A.P.M.S. 6th Division about getting straw at BOIS GRENIER thrashed before use.	fras

Helen M Miller Major
O.C. 19th hf. Div. Train.

131/4893

XIX Infantry Brigade. Train.

Volume 1 — 31.3.15

Army Form C. 2118.

WAR DIARY
or
INTELLIGENCE SUMMARY. XIX hd Bde Train

(Erase heading not required.)

Instructions regarding War Diaries and Intelligence
Summaries are contained in F.S. Regs., Part II.
and the Staff Manual respectively. Title pages
will be prepared in manuscript.

Hour, Date, Place	Summary of Events and Information	Remarks and references to Appendices
LES 3 TILLEULS, FRANCE 1-3-15	Made arrangements to have Lethargic Shaw of BOIS GRENIER taken back to 1 ARMEE + Picked Rene Bread + groceries which had been ordered today. Officials made good from Stock at Railhead.	yes
2-3-15	Major-General Sir I.K.W. K.C.B, G.O.C. 6th Division inspected all the transport of the Bde. He went to all files had him at the Reg Coal crossing on the ARMENTIERES – ERQUINGHEM road. 1st line vehicles all went first + Train came last. He expressed himself as well satisfied with condition of horses & vehicles.	yes
3-3-15	Dr. O'Callaghan admitted to HP. Interviewed A.A.Q.M.G. 6th Division re Parking of Shaw at BOIS GRENIER, as G.O.C. 19th A.B.; Bde will not allow it to be hampered in any account of the noise made by the vehicles. Also Parking of BOIS GRENIER and the lines. Saddl. Sgt. E. Clegg + Dr. Carter returned from leave this morning. Pte Loathead transferred to 4 Coy; 6th Divl. Train.	yes
4-3-15	Inspected horses of Regt. except 1st Scottish Rifles Ammunition Column.	yes
5-3-15	Inspected horses of 1st S.J. Rifles Ammunition Column. Board of Officers to value charger of Capt. C.T. Heywood, at 2-in-1 Res B.D. Stranger valued at £70. Interviewed O.C. 17th Field Ambulance with view to getting use of forge here for one of 1st line transport. He has no objection provided we supply the coal, + clean up the place after use. Fixed days for the different units to satisfied Bde Transport Officer yes. Had parade this afternoon for instruction in firing annual exercises.	yes

Army Form C. 2118.

WAR DIARY
or
INTELLIGENCE SUMMARY. XIX h/f 1B&T Team

(Erase heading not required.)

Instructions regarding War Diaries and Intelligence Summaries are contained in F.S. Regs., Part II. and the Staff Manual respectively. Title pages will be prepared in manuscript.

Hour, Date, Place	Summary of Events and Information	Remarks and references to Appendices
LES 3 TILLEULS, FRANCE 6-3-15	2/Lt. H. McLellan returned from leave this morning. Attended conference of S/offs officers at Coys HQ. Lt Redfern O/C Cleaner 6th Division, inspected damage done to his Factory by his men there during their occupation.	
7-3-15	Requisitioned handcarts for use by Coy Repts. to take rations up to the trenches.	gas
8-3-15	A bitterly cold day with N.E. wind & some snow. Pt Rivers missed from 27th Divis. Supply Coln. Cpl. Drayton admitted to H.P. Had instruction in firing manual exercises for the men for an hour this afternoon. Received instruction that Head at BOIS GRENIER is not now to be	gas
9-3-15	Presented, nor too it to be registered. 1 L.B. have sent to 1st Commanders.	gas
10-3-15	Rendered Confidential report on Temporary Commissioned Officers, Lt A Buchanan & 2/Lt. B.V.H. McLellan & 2/D Adjt. 1st Army. Recommended both to humanise breast difficulty rent. Instructions received from Bde HQ. that no officer or other rank is to leave his billeting area, except when on duty, without previous reference to Bde HQ. Inspected horses of 1st line transport.	gas
11-3-15	Saddlers of 1st Sjt. Rifles. Had test checking up of wagons & getting everything ready to move off. We could be clear of his billet under 1½ hours.	gas

(73969) W4141—463. 400,000. 9/14. H.&J.Ltd. Forms/C. 2118/10.

Army Form C. 2118.

WAR DIARY
or
INTELLIGENCE SUMMARY. XIX h.f. 13 de T rein

(Erase heading not required.)

Instructions regarding War Diaries and Intelligence Summaries are contained in F.S. Regs., Part II and the Staff Manual respectively. Title pages will be prepared in manuscript.

Hour, Date, Place	Summary of Events and Information	Remarks and references to Appendices
LES 3 TILLEULS, FRANCE 12-3-15	Had water tanks of billet filled again. Cpl. Draper returned from Fr. Went to ESTAIRES to see manager of Brewery concerning Requisition Receipt for coke & coal which we had taken from the ARMENTIERES Breweries, as he cannot agree on a reasonable price to be paid & H.Q. forwarded instructions not a Receipt note should be given.	fbs
13-3-15	A H.D. horses received from 6 Divs: Train & 1 Riding from 13th H.Q. Supplies to requirements none. Attended Conference of M.M.L.O. Officers at 3rd Corps H.Q. 1/Middlesex Regt. took over Right Section of line held by 16th h.f. 13 de bright.	fbs
14-3-15	Got 6 tons coke & 107 sacks charcoal from Railhead.	fbs
15-3-15	Got 6 more tons of coke & 23 sacks charcoal from Railhead HQ. Lt Bicheller Was in charge of convoys. The field beside the billet is sufficiently dry now to have drills on it. & had a football this afternoon, at which I gave no 3 trade NCO's & practice in drilling. Considering the fact that men are Reservists who have been away from the Colours for years the result was most creditable.	fbs
16-3-15	Horses turned out to graze instead of going out for exercise along roads.	fbs

(73989) W4141—463. 400,000. 9/14. H.&J.Ltd. Forms/C. 2118/10.

WAR DIARY or INTELLIGENCE SUMMARY.

XIV Inf. Bde. Train

Army Form C. 2118.

(Erase heading not required.)

Hour, Date, Place	Summary of Events and Information	Remarks and references to Appendices
LES 3 TILLEULS, FRANCE 17-3-15	Frost makes its first appearance for many months on this road. Inspected horses, harness, saddlery, & vehicles of Ammunition Column, 1st Line Transport of 2/A.&S.Hdrs, 1/Middlesex & 5th Scottish Rifles. Various minor repairs are required and instructions were given for the articles in question to be sent to Train A.P. for repair. Buckles of nearly all S.A.A. Carts & G.S. limbered wagons are nearly all chipped with grease immovable. Gave orders that oil was to be used in future instead of grease. Received telegram from D.D.f.S.T. 2nd Army to hire K.A.S.C. Records at B.H.S.E. names of N.C.O.s for Home. Recommended the following:- C.S.M. Peddler, S/Sgt Bean A.C.P.S., Sgts. Cahill & Sanderson, Cpl. Gilbert, Prov. Cpls. Ferguson & Bamford, Pion: 1st & Cpls. Williamson, Matthews.	
18-3-15	Inspected horses, harness, saddlers, & vehicles of this transport of 2/A.R. held Frailers & the Cameronians found same results as yesterday. In compliance with a wire from D.S.C. Records at BASE, sent off this afternoon from Railhead the following N.C.O.s & men to BASE COMMANDANT at HAVRE en route for home :- Sgts. Cahill Sanderson, Cpl. Gilbert, Prov. Cpls. Ferguson & Bamford. Sent Pion: Sgt. Clark to Field Ambulance to replace Sgt. Sanderson.	

WAR DIARY
or
INTELLIGENCE SUMMARY. XIX H.Q. D.P. Train.

Army Form C. 2118.

Hour, Date, Place	Summary of Events and Information	Remarks and references to Appendices
LES 3 TILLEULS, FRANCE 18-3-15	Pte W.R. R.P. Smith, suppla to establishment, was sent to Base & 4 days, in compliance with order received from D.D. of S.T., II Army. Notification received from Base H.Q. that orders issued on 10th inst. restricting officers from taking billetting areas was cancelled.	Yes.
19-3-15	Another change in the weather. Very cold & Footprints. Inspected horses, harness, saddlery & vehicles of T/3 Co Co. D.P. Condition on the whole good. Several minor repairs to harness in regt., & R.I.O.A. I have ordered to be carried out at once. Having received their travelling kitchen, their cooker vehicle was available for return & orders issued for men to be disposed of as follows :— 2/R. Welsh Fusiliers to Train to replace 2 civilian wagons for 5th Scottish Rifles, 1/Cameronians to 5th Scottish Rifles to replace 2 civilian wagons, 1/Middlesex to 2/A.S. Hptrs to replace a blanket cart which is unserviceable. 2/R.W.F. sent 4 H.D. horses + 2 G.S. wagons to Train this afternoon. H.D.	
20-3-15	2 Civilian wagons & 2 horses rec'd from 5/Scottish Rifles, on receipt of G.S. wagon from 1/Cameronians. Other 2 horses of cooks vehicle returned to 1/Cameronians to make up deficiencies. 1 Blanket cart + 1 horse received from 2/A.A.S. Hptrs on receipt of G.S. wagon from 1/Middlesex Regt. One horse retained by 2/A.S. Hptrs to make up deficiency.	

Army Form C. 2118.

WAR DIARY
~~INTELLIGENCE SUMMARY~~ XIX Aff 13 & T rain
(Erase heading not required.)

Instructions regarding War Diaries and Intelligence Summaries are contained in F.S. Regs., Part II. and the Staff Manual respectively. Title pages will be prepared in manuscript.

Hour, Date, Place	Summary of Events and Information	Remarks and references to Appendices
LES 3 TILLEULS, FRANCE 20-3-15	Supply wagon for Train sent to Refilling Point to draw supplies for Regts. with Travelling Kitchens. Visited Railhead & attended conference of S.O. at 8th Corps H.Q. N. & S. Midland Territorial Division arrived today & 6th N. Staffords are attached to this Bde. Have arranged to supply men with fruit, stew, fresh vegetables & per soap, other supplies being drawn range reis on supply officers I.L.D. have to field ambulance to replace wastage. I.H.D. to mobile reserve section	yes.
21-3-15	As supply wagon have now to go to Regts, owing to withdrawal of cook'd vehicles, Refilling Point changed today to LES 3 TILLEULS wagons returned to billet after refilling went up to trench at 3 p.m. These with kitchens, returned supply wagons to take rations into firing line & did not get back till 11 p.m. Sent to Railhead for return 1 blanket cart & 2 civilian wagons & left of civilian wagons to go to A. Ahmed Base H.T. Depot. These for HAVRE were despatched tonight but no facilities for sending horses, which were returned, stabled for night at STEENWERCK. Wire received from O.C. tonight to stop despatch of these wagons, but it was too late to stop rare for HAVRE. Leat motor car to Pres. H.M. Nell. Peploe,	

Army Form C. 2118.

WAR DIARY
or
INTELLIGENCE SUMMARY. XIX from 18 to 7 am

(Erase heading not required.)

Hour, Date, Place	Summary of Events and Information	Remarks and references to Appendices
LES 3 TILLEULS, FRANCE 21-3-15	Lewin C. of E. Chaplain, 6th Division, to enable him to carry out all his services today. As he would otherwise have had to have cancelled if he had not been able to get loan of a car. He told me in his billet for the train in afternoon. 2/Lt. Hicks arrived today from MEERUT Supply Column. Got drunk as usual. About 10.15 p.m. detected Gunner Jones, 68th Bty., R.F.A. attempting to steal a sack of marmalade tarts, awaiting return to the BASE for ophira. Handed him over to A.P.M. 4th Division.	f/25. f/25.
22-3-15	System of giving temporary receipts for articles requisitioned ceases from today inclusive. All articles required to be requisitioned will be obtained by stand for or applied to Requisitioning officer in future. The 2 complete horses sent to STEENWERCK yesterday, returned. Supply wagon, after refilling, went direct to 1st line tranches. Those with who are in billet, distributed their rations fortnight & empties reprovisioned to Train H.Q. In the case of units who are in the tranches, the wagons are left at end of line the horses return to Train H.Q. Reg 80 up in return about 6 p.m. to make return to the tranches (as near as possible) return to Train H.Q. on completion. Obtained 1/2 qrs of charcoal from STEENWERCK. Received 6 kms of coffee & 4 kms of charcoal from STEENWERCK. 2/Lt. A. H. Oakenham was in charge of convoy.	f/25.

WAR DIARY
INTELLIGENCE SUMMARY. XIX h/1 B.S. Train

Army Form C. 2118.

(Erase heading not required.)

Hour, Date, Place	Summary of Events and Information	Remarks and references to Appendices
LES TILLEULS, FRANCE. 23-3-15	O.C. 6th Div. Train inspected 2 horses not returned for Railhead yesterday. Been instruction for one to be sent to 1 Co; 6th Div. Train, which was done. Other wagon sent to Railhead to be returned to C.O.O. HAVRE; 2 horses returned meanwhile.	
24-3-15.	Inspected horses of Field ambulance, who have now moved to ERQUINGHEM; also those of Amm: Colm; 1/Middlesex; 1/Cameronians; 2/R. Irish Fusiliers + 2/A.+S. Hdrs. Travelling kitchen was received today by 2/A.+S. Hdrs. 1st 2nd Scottish Rifles & the 1/Middlesex Regt. Received 2 to complete Rein. 1 H.D. horse and no Installation Section with paralysis in hind quarter. 1 Blanket cart rec'd from 1/Middlesex Regt on receipt of 2 travelling kitchens. 1 H.D. horse returned to complete establishment of 9 H.D. Res Sec. 1 H.D. deficient as had no horse to return with Blanket cart. 1 H.D. horse, 1 civilian + 1 G.S. wagon received from 5th Scottish Rifles.	yes.
25-3-15.	Inspected horses of 5th Scottish Rifles. Dispatched men to return 2 G.S. wagons + 4 H.D. horses in addition to those returned yesterday, as has had 4 wagons for escorts instead of only 2. This number is in afternoon. One officer & 8 men were sent to 1/Cameronians in lieu of Blanket cart. 1 H.D. horse to Field ambulance to replace casualty.	yes.
26-3-15.	2/A.+S. Hdrs returned to 1/Middlesex Regt. re G.S. wagon, was rec'd from Rein. on 19th inst. The 1/Middlesex returned to the Rein. 2 2nd	

WAR DIARY
or
INTELLIGENCE SUMMARY. XIX h/q/B₂ Train

Army Form C. 2118.

(Erase heading not required.)

Hour, Date, Place	Summary of Events and Information	Remarks and references to Appendices
LES 3 TILLEULS, FRANCE 26-3-15	Blanket cart: 2/A.T.D. returned with rain coats vehicle & Blanket wagon returned to me & the rain Blanket cart & 3 H.D. knives, returning. O/C H.D. Ox Rein /spare A.D. to complete men establishment. 1.S. wagon took VIII from 5ᵗʰ Scottish Rifles and 1/Cameronians, who returned rain 2 Blanket carts to me. 1 G.S. wagon from 5ᵗʰ Scottish Rifles also to 2/R. Welch Fusiliers in lieu of Blanket cart to be returned home. 1 L.D. horse to 1/Middlesex Regt to replace casualty. JAS.	
27-3-15	Blanket cart received from 2.R.W. Fusiliers. Visited Railhead & attended conference of Supply officers at 3ʳᵈ Corps H.Q. Payment for 6ᵗʰ Div: Postie & homeles handed over to us & 1/8ᵗʰ h/q.B₂. R.O. 1 Run Hut 19ᵗʰ Field ambulance has taken him over from Pte 18ᵗʰ. An excellent performance was given tonight by 6ᵗʰ Div: Fancies, which was attended by B'goo C 3ʳᵈ Corps & 6 C Div:, to which we also went. JAS.	
28-3-15	O.C. 6ᵗʰ Div: Train inspected Blanket carts Horses which here returned on above from waits. After inspection sent 6 carts & 1 Civilian wagon to STEENWERCK to be returned to C.O.O., HAVRE. 2 L.D. horses received from Ammn: Colm: in lieu of 1 M.D. Stranded over to 1/Middlesex Regt. to replace casualties. 6 H.D. horses to 1 Co3: 6 C Div: Train ; 1 H.D. horse to 6ᵗʰ Mobile Veterinary Section – pregnancy. 1 H.D. horse to 1/Cameronians to replace casualty. JAS.	

Army Form C. 2118.

WAR DIARY
or
INTELLIGENCE SUMMARY. XIX 7/13th Train
(Erase heading not required.)

Instructions regarding War Diaries and Intelligence Summaries are contained in F.S. Regs., Part II. and the Staff Manual respectively. Title pages will be prepared in manuscript.

Hour, Date, Place	Summary of Events and Information	Remarks and references to Appendices
LES TILLEULS, FRANCE 29-3-15.	1 horse cart & 1 L.D. horse from Bde H.Q., surplus to authorized establishment. 1 L.D. horse to 2/A.A. Hqtrs to replace casualty. Dvr Harris + Manning transferring to 2/A.A. Hqtrs for Blanket Hygiene. Dvr Phillips to 19th Field Ambulance vice Dvr Flothers to BASE H.P.	gas.
30-3-15.	Issue of another – about 4.00 lbs – made today. Inspection made by 6th Div: to to go to different billets on account of crossing of lines of supply. Decision arrived at not to change at present.	gas.
31-3-15.	Men sent from Bde H.Q. sent to 1 Cav: 6th Div: Train. Bishop of London gave an address to the men of this Brigade in schoolroom at L'ARMEE at 3.15. Form filled up anything.	gas.

[signature]
O.C. 19th 7/13 d. Train.

(73989) W4141—463. 400,000. 9/14. H.&J. Ltd. Forms/C. 2118/10.

121/5255

19th Brigade Train
Vol IX 1 – 30.4.15

Army Form C. 2118.

WAR DIARY
or
INTELLIGENCE SUMMARY. XX Infl 2 Train

(Erase heading not required.)

Instructions regarding War Diaries and Intelligence Summaries are contained in F.S. Regs., Part II and the Staff Manual respectively. Title pages will be prepared in manuscript.

Hour, Date, Place	Summary of Events and Information	Remarks and references to Appendices
LES 3 TILLEULS, FRANCE 1-4-15	B.W.H.Q. moved to L'ARMEÉ. 5th & 8th Royal Warwickshire Regt. received todays & are attached to this B?. They are to be applied by me with Fuel, Straw & fresh vegetables.	yes
2-4-15	Sold 1695 kilos of old horse shoes at 2.5fr: per kilog. Dr. Atkinson F. transferred to Base H.P.	yes
3-4-15	Attended conference of Supply officers at 3rd Corps H.Q. D.C.C.'s Divn: Train inspected all bicycles this afternoon at his H.Q.	yes
4-4-15	Lent car to Rev: held Peploe to enable him to go from one billet to another to give his services. In afternoon he held one in Train billet, which was fairly well attended. Holy Communion was administered after the service.	yes
5-4-15	Lt Irwin A.V.C. handed over Veterinary charge of this B? to Lt Hill. all common transfer returns in accordance with orders, rendered certificate today that how are now more in possession of this Unit. Privs: Newrood, Waltars, Winch, Webb, Wood, Walker & Nakes arrived from Base H.T. Depot Privates S. + C.S. F.W. Potter Abl. Farrier Corpl. to complete establishment.	yes

Army Form C. 2118.

WAR DIARY
or
INTELLIGENCE SUMMARY. XIX Inf. Bde Train

(Erase heading not required.)

Instructions regarding War Diaries and Intelligence Summaries are contained in F. S. Regs., Part II. and the Staff Manual respectively. Title pages will be prepared in manuscript.

Hour, Date, Place	Summary of Events and Information	Remarks and references to Appendices
LES 3 TILLEULS, FRANCE 6-4-15	Sr. Wrote to 19th Field Ambulance 1 class of 6th Div. Horse Show held in ARMENTIERES. Entered horses for best light draught pair & wagon; Best heavy draught pair & wagon; Best team of four and wagon; but none of them were placed. Lt. Butenshaw went to BRUAY to arrange about despatch of steam coal for 6th Bris. Baths. 5th & 6th Bde Royal Warwickshire Regt. left holes.	
7-4-15	2. class of Horse Show. Entered for Best Heavy Draught, Best Light Draught, Best trust horse up to 12 Stone, Best trust horse up to 14 Stone, but none were placed.	gas
6-4-15	Motor car left in sides for general overhaul & cleaning. Inspected horses of 1/Cameronian Field Ambulance. Supply Column dumped 3 lorry loads of Supplies, as there was a lot of shave coke to be brought from Railhead, which necessitated a 2nd journey. Baths at billet was filled again.	gas
9-4-15	20 tons steam coal arrived at ARMENTIERES ANNEXE for 6th Bris. Baths & was carted next holes. Re west Edge dying harness. Inspected, live transport of 1/Middlesex Regt. & horses of ammunition Column, 2/A.T.S. Adm, 2/R.W. Fusiliers. The Germans shelled the billets of Ammunition Column about 11 am, but did no damage	gas

Army Form C. 2118.

WAR DIARY
or
INTELLIGENCE SUMMARY. XIX 7/f 13th Train

(Erase heading not required.)

Instructions regarding War Diaries and Intelligence Summaries are contained in F. S. Regs., Part II. and the Staff Manual respectively. Title pages will be prepared in manuscript.

Hour, Date, Place	Summary of Events and Information	Remarks and references to Appendices
LES 3 TILLEULS, FRANCE 9-4-15	except to one horse close by, Rene May killed an old man some of our waggons had a narrow escape as they were passing at the time. + Boy hall went over Rev. Bang of the Shells were blind. much can effect again for cleaning it.	fars
10-4-15	H.Q. p/2 off No Gloucester + November 13th + 8 C.13? Lincolnshire Regt. arrived today were attached to this B.Q. 3 W. Corps H.Q. to attend conference of Supply Officers. Brig. Hill, Holland, Hawker, Tapke, + Moss arrived from base H.T. Depot. Had smoking concert in men's billet tonight. Most successful, with assistance from Re Follies, who are only too pleased to be able to do something at these concerts.	fars
11-4-15.	No memorable received notes. 1 Riding horse to 20.6 Mobile Veterinary Section - pregnancy. Br: S. de. Enfield appointed acting Scale Corpl. to complete establishment	fars.
12-4-15.	Suggested to A.C.G.p.m.B. 6th Division Return form a Tennis Club for Officers of the Division attached Troops, at Re ARMENTIERES. Tennis Club. He said he would ask the G.O.C. about it.	fars.

(73989) W4141—463. 400,000. 9/14. H.&J.Ltd. Forms/C. 2118/10.

Army Form C. 2118.

WAR DIARY
or
INTELLIGENCE SUMMARY. XIX Corps Supply & Train.

(Erase heading not required.)

Instructions regarding War Diaries and Intelligence Summaries are contained in F.S. Regs., Part II. and the Staff Manual respectively. Title pages will be prepared in manuscript.

Hour, Date, Place	Summary of Events and Information	Remarks and references to Appendices
LES 3 TILLEULS, FRANCE 12-4-15	Received 1 Country Cart from 6th Div. Train, to carry forage.	
13-4-15	Went to BRUAY Mines to arrange about sending up to Army S. team coal for 6th Division. The Manager of the Mines will not guarantee a weekly supply - it is necessary to go down there every time a truck equipment is required.	Jas.
14-4-15	Arranged with M. Motte, President of the ARMENTIERES Tennis Club to take over his courts.	Jas.
15-4-15	Supply Column dumped 3 lorry loads of hay. Railhead & took 3 loads of straw. Gen. Kerr consented to the formation of the Tennis Club. Had first meeting tonight & elected a Committee.	Jas.
16-4-15	Lt. Seymour, O/c Branch Regulating Office 201. Came this evening to investigate the amounts of coal & coke which had been requisitioned from the ARMENTIERES Gas Works.	Jas.
17-4-15	Visited Railhead & attended conference of Supply Officers at 3rd Corps H.Q. Asked for 200 lbs. of flour to be sent up daily in lieu of biscuit; also for meat ration to be made up as follows:- 3500 rations frozen meat, 1000 preserved + 1000 M. + V.	Jas.

(73989) W4141—463. 400,000. 9/14. H.&J.Ltd. Forms/C. 2118/10.

WAR DIARY
or
INTELLIGENCE SUMMARY. XIX H.Q. f.B. & Train

Army Form C. 2118.

(Erase heading not required.)

Instructions regarding War Diaries and Intelligence Summaries are contained in F.S. Regs., Part II. and the Staff Manual respectively. Title pages will be prepared in manuscript.

Hour, Date, Place	Summary of Events and Information	Remarks and references to Appendices
3 TILLEULS, FRANCE 17-4-15		
18-4-15	Dvr Frampton, H/Q & Weaver rejoined from BASE. H.T. Depot. Gloucester Doncaster B/Co left Valley. 1 Riding Horse rec'd from 1 Cavalry Div. Inspected lines of Field Ambulance. Gradient & Steering gear of motor car broke this morning. Car was removed to Supply Column Workshops & new gradient wired for.	Yes. Yes.
19-4-15	Wrote billet of J.S.O. 6th Div. Went & met L' Symms together. He went through negotiations for coal worker replenished from ARMENTIERS grounds. Started work marches for the Company + Lt Robertson took him for 6 mile march. Lt Bainbridge Jr. Dismissed man of L.O. Section. Lieut. Stewer Sgt Standrige Jr.	Yes.
20-4-15	Mention in despatches for good work done since beginning of the year. Lt Mitchellen took Company for a 5 mile Route March this afternoon. Corked hams were received today for first time in lieu of portion of ordinary bacon. Does no notice good as the bacon we usually get.	Yes.
21-4-15	Inspected transport of No 84 HQ. One tool wagon is badly in need of repairs & Motor were given to HQs to send to the Train to be repaired. Received first consignment of envelopes for letters & family letters only which need not be censored regimentally.	Yes. Yes.

(73989) W4141-463. 400,000. 9/14. H.&J.Ltd. Forms/C. 2118/10.

WAR DIARY
or
INTELLIGENCE SUMMARY. XIX H.Q. 13th Train

Army Form C. 2118.

(Erase heading not required.)

Hour, Date, Place	Summary of Events and Information	Remarks and references to Appendices
LES 3 TILLEULS, FRANCE 22-4-15.	Lt. Mahon from 19th Field Ambulance inspected horses of all Regts., Field Ambulance, Column. Appointed R.S.M. Begay, M.S. Corps to complete establishment. First issue of flour in lieu of biscuit — 196 lbs; also of horse in place of	yes
23-4-15.	2.03: In lieu of 1st & 3rd gun, trooped & small proportion of gun vans. Inspected farms, view to proposed to billet at Train next month. Supply Column had 12 tons of stores to bring up; 1.30 hrs dumped all the supplies this afternoon & refilled again this evening instead of tomorrow morning. Lt. Weaver to 19th Field Ambulance. 2 H.D. Lorries received from 19th Field Ambulance May 2nd/03; 6 D Div Train to complete establishment. Field Ambulance received 7 motor ambulances yesterday in lieu of 7 horsed vehicles. Lt. Pakenham took Company to Route march this afternoon to 3rd Corps H.Q. where sent with S.S.O. 6th Div; to Railhead stes. to Railhead.	yes
24-4-15	He attended conference of MT Officers. Suggested that circle Paraffin be issued on a divisional indent. Asked for 1300 Ration of tinned meat & beans to be sent up daily.	yes

WAR DIARY
or
~~INTELLIGENCE SUMMARY~~ XIX 7/13ᵈ Train

Army Form C. 2118.

(Erase heading not required.)

Hour, Date, Place	Summary of Events and Information	Remarks and references to Appendices
LES 3 TILLEULS, FRANCE 25-4-15	Settled into train at NIEPPE for billets from 1/3/15 to 24/4/15 inclusive. 2 H.D. horses received from 4 Coy: 6 Cʸ. Sup̄. Train.	JBS.
26-4-15	Supply Column arrived at 7 a.m. as it was to be at Railhead by 8.30 a.m. daily in future. Lt Henderson + 2ⁿᵈ Lieutenant took company for Route march this afternoon. Sgt Bonneval proceeded to-day to D.D.T., H.Q., I.S.C. in accordance with wire received from A.S.C. Records yesterday. Held muster parade, concert tonight, chaplain Lt Hill A.V.C. rendered valuable assistance.	JBS.
27-4-15	Gen. t ei opened the Tennis Club for officers of the Division and attached troops this afternoon. Gun Lingard & Lambourne arrived from BADF H.T. depôt	JBS.
28-4-15	Purchased a ton of coal for 5th Div: laundry, 5 tons for the Rubber + H for the Troops from ARMENTIERES. Gas works on rare had come up in a rail. J. Supply Coln. dumped 3 lorry loads of supplies this afternoon & returned to railhead to pick up stores. Lt Pakenham took company for route march this afternoon	JBS.

Army Form C. 2118.

WAR DIARY
~~INTELLIGENCE SUMMARY~~ XIX Inf. Bde Train
(Erase heading not required.)

Instructions regarding War Diaries and Intelligence Summaries are contained in F.S. Regs., Part II and the Staff Manual respectively. Title pages will be prepared in manuscript.

Hour, Date, Place	Summary of Events and Information	Remarks and references to Appendices
LES 3 TILLEULS, FRANCE 29-4-15	Inspected Horse transport of 1st Middlesex Regt. & the lines of the Other unifs. & Field ambulance & Ammunition Column.	Yes.
30-4-15	Inspected horses & billets in ERQUINGHEM of Supply Detachment & Ambulance to 19th Inf. Bde. Ammunition Column. Famil. Cople. Porter to Field Ambulance in relief of S/Sgt. S. Allchin, who returned to Train. Stratteffe.	Yes.

Colin M. Micklem Major
O.C. 19th Inf. Bde. Train.

121/55/3

19th Brigade

19th Bde: Train

Army Form C. 2118.

WAR DIARY
or
INTELLIGENCE SUMMARY. XIX Afect Train

(Erase heading not required.)

Instructions regarding War Diaries and Intelligence Summaries are contained in F.S. Regs., Part II. and the Staff Manual respectively. Title pages will be prepared in manuscript.

Hour, Date, Place	Summary of Events and Information	Remarks and references to Appendices
LES 3 TILLEULS, FRANCE 1-5-15	Went to Railhead France to 3rd Corps H.Q., Were attended Conference of S.S.O. – Asked for additional 1 gallon of Cresoli to be sent up daily.	
	O/c Loets arrived from B.A.E H.T. Depot.	Yes.
2-5-15	Inspected Billets in ERQUINGHEM-LYS & decided on move for the supply & detachment.	Yes.
	2nd yoff joined from B.A.E H.T. Depot.	
ERQUINGHEM-LYS 3-5-15	Train moved from present billet under orders from 6th Division & went to farm of M. MEAUX GRUSON, about a mile further S. along road to CROIX DU BAC, & close to the river LYS. Supplies detachment moved to ERQUINGHEM-LYS, beside new the Refilling Point to be from Amanouinchosive. Train H.Q. in RUE DE L'AVENIR, ERQUINGHEM-LYS. The horses wagons are in the open in 2 separate fields. Passed a wet night for their first night, but no harm resulted. Most of the men prefer sleeping in bivouacs to being in the barn.	MSC.

Army Form C. 2118.

WAR DIARY
or
INTELLIGENCE SUMMARY. XIX hq 13th co Train

(Erase heading not required.)

Hour, Date, Place	Summary of Events and Information	Remarks and references to Appendices
ERQUINGHEM - LYS 4-3-15 May	Refilling Point changed to ERQUINGHEM in the side road by the Church & not off the main road. Quite a suitable & convenient place. Column arrived about 7.30 Sundays & Supply Train wagons came along about 9, refill & so straight to their units. Bright sunshine today som died up the ground after the rain during the night.	JAS.
5-3-15	Got severe orders for the latrine made, and the basin for the men to wash in.	JAS.
6-3-15	Got Cordin from R.E. for washing basin & Rd suitable drain & pit dug for dirty water. Major Gen. Sir J. Keir K.C.B., G.O.C. 6th Div. in company with Brig: Gen. Sir F. Gordon Bro., inspected the billets & the horses. This evening expressed himself as very well satisfied. Inspected horses & fell in at Lime Transport ammunition column & Rum all looking very fit. ARMENTIERES was heavily shelled this morning between 6 a.m & 7 a.m., many shell dropping in & now: Refilling Point which has now been moved to CROIX DU BAC. Not much damage was done. One of the drivers - Pte Hall - attacked by the H.Q. was hit by Shrapnel in his leg & had to go to hospital.	JAS.

WAR DIARY
or
INTELLIGENCE SUMMARY. XIX Infantry Bde. Train.

(Erase heading not required.)

Army Form C. 2118.

Instructions regarding War Diaries and Intelligence Summaries are contained in F. S. Regs., Part II. and the Staff Manual respectively. Title pages will be prepared in manuscript.

Hour, Date, Place		Summary of Events and Information	Remarks and references to Appendices
ERQUINGHEM – LYS 7-5-15		Inspected horses of No. 19th Field Ambulance. Lt. Graham to Bde HQ. vice Lt. Hall wounded yesterday.	fras.
8-5-15		Visited Railhead & then on to 3rd Corps H.Q. where I attended conference of S.S.O. Canadian Division have now come back to 3rd Corps. Same meeting at STEENWERCK. Refreshed at Lapenne or ADVANCE Branch of Preserved Meat made by JULZBERGER, CHICAGO, that all knit complain of its palatability, being salt – tasting with a large amount of gristle. Lt. Parkenham took Company for Route March this afternoon. Lt. Capt. Williamson to BASE Hospital.	fras.
9-5-15	R	Got 25000 kilos of ration from BOIS GRENIER at 5.F. 100 kilos sun winsh & Lapate to 19th Field Ambulance in relief of dum. Flynn & Phill who have been getting into trouble, when re B.O.C. of this Bde. requested me to take back to No. 1 train. 2nd Lt. Edgell Pakenham promoted to T/Lieut d/- 1/5/15.	fras.
10-5-15	R	Checked receipt of A. Bn. 64 bree rot bags one correctly entered up shipments kept.	fras.

Army Form C. 2118.

WAR DIARY
or
INTELLIGENCE SUMMARY 7th/B. 2. T.m.
(Erase heading not required.)

Instructions regarding War Diaries and Intelligence Summaries are contained in F.S. Regs., Part II. and the Staff Manual respectively. Title pages will be prepared in manuscript.

Hour, Date, Place	Summary of Events and Information	Remarks and references to Appendices
ERQUINGHEM - LYS		
10-5-15	Battery particulars sent. Purchased 400 kilos of Chloride of lime as there has been a shortage lately. To disinfectants of any kind came up today, no diminished Chloride of lime purchased yesterday.	JBS
12-5-15	Rt. Revd. The Bishop of Pretoria D.D gave an address in R.J Bartroom at L'ARMEE this afternoon. 4/Cpl. Millar, clerk, arrived today from RAE H.T. Depot.	JBS
13-5-15	Issued 474 gallons of crude paraffin, received 1560z as disinfectant. Inspected 1st Divn. Transport lines of all Regts. & Ammunition Coln. Also disinfected vehicles, harness etc. of 5th R.S. Rifles & the Cameronians. Recommended Lt. J.A. Edgell to be promoted Lieutenant, in reply to query from HQrs 2nd Army. The Bridge over the LYS was closed to all wheeled traffic this evening. Left wagons by roadside on the S. side of the river, or return from units & the horses were allowed to go over the Bridge. The road as far as L'Epinette Cross Roads is closed for repair.	
14-5-15	Arranged for wagons in future to be parked in RUE de L'AVENIR, Beside Hop. Billet, the horses to go over the bridge only & back to their billets. The Bishop of Pretoria gave another address this afternoon in	JBS

WAR DIARY
or
INTELLIGENCE SUMMARY. XIX A/13 C Train

(Erase heading not required.)

Army Form C. 2118.

Hour, Date, Place		Summary of Events and Information	Remarks and references to Appendices
ERQUINGHEM - LYS 14-5-15	R	in the l'ARMEE Schoolroom, and a detachment from the Train attended. Proto car returned today. No new gradient has yet been received from the BASE, but owing to arrival of some Blacksmiths the O.C. Suppl. Col. was able to have a new one forged, which is much stronger than the last.	JBS.
15-5-15	R	Went to Railhead & hence to Corps H.Q. Were attended Conference of Supply Officers, shortage in weight of bread reported. Handed sparks office to 16th, 117th, 118th & 19th Field Ambulances	JBS.
16-5-15		2/Lt. Hicks applied leave, sent to 1 Coy: 6th Div: Train.	JBS.
17-5-15		9th Division. The first of the new armies to arrive here, came into this area in afternoon	JBS.
18-5-15	R	Chloride of lime came up again. Inspected horses of Field Ambulances	JBS.
19-5-15	R	Inspected all transport of 2/R. Welsh Fusiliers, 2/A.S. Highrs, recommended flannel shirts and drawers by 1/Cameronian/Middlesex 15th J. with or Rifles.	JBS.
20-5-15		Supply Column moved into billets in ARMENTIERES. Tomorrow's supplies were dumped this afternoon & train refilled second time at 4P.M.	JBS.

WAR DIARY
or
INTELLIGENCE SUMMARY. XIX hf B.W. Train

Army Form C. 2118.

(Erase heading not required.)

Instructions regarding War Diaries and Intelligence Summaries are contained in F.S. Regs., Part II and the Staff Manual respectively. Title pages will be prepared in manuscript.

Hour, Date, Place	Summary of Events and Information	Remarks and references to Appendices
ERQUINGHEM - LYS 21-5-15	No Supplies/Credit Depôts received. Inspected horses of ammunition column. 1 H.D. horse discharged by veterinary officer. 1 Riding horse to 1/Cameronians. 1 list A. Buchanan promoted 2nd H.D. horses to 1/Middlesex Regt. as L.D. Temp: Capt d/-26/3/15. T. Lt A.V.H. Mikelly promoted T. Lieut d/ 20/3/15	JBS.
22-5-15	Attended Conference of S.S.O.s at 3rd Corps H.Q., also via S.S.O. of 9th Division attended for 1st time.	JBS.
23-5-15	Camera returned today for a second time in accordance with orders. Not all are to be sent home again. Certificate rendered to HQ that this had been done.	JBS.
24-5-15	a/ waster Capt. A. W. Bothing tried by F.G.C.M. for returning from duty drunk on the afternoon of 19th inst. Lt. Pakenham prosecuted. 1 Riding horse Remount received today. Infantile not up to much being broken-winded & with near fore knee broken. St. Holland to 19th Field Ambulance vice A'haker to BASE IP. Lt. Edgell today handed over Supply duties to T. Capt. A. Buchanan, who in his turn handed over Requisitioning duties to Lt. Edgell.	JBS.
25-5-15		

Army Form C. 2118.

WAR DIARY
or
INTELLIGENCE SUMMARY. XIX h/q Bty R.C.H.A.

(Erase heading not required.)

Instructions regarding War Diaries and Intelligence Summaries are contained in F. S. Regs., Part II. and the Staff Manual respectively. Title pages will be prepared in manuscript.

Hour, Date, Place	Summary of Events and Information	Remarks and references to Appendices
ERQUINGHEM – LYS 25 – 5 –15	Lt Gilkson relieved 2/Lt Beattie I/c pair of 1st Cavalry Wagon horses of 1 Canadians	
26 – 5 – 15	F.B.C.M. proceeding in cease of G.A.E. Capt. Rothing promoted. Horses considered to be reduced to the ranks. Gale performance of the "Fancies". Lt McKellen reached 4.0 of the Company in Lt. Lt Miller admitted to H.P., Broken leg.	yes.
27 – 5 – 15	When the supply wagons of the 2/R Welsh Fusiliers were returning from delivering the rations, about 10 P.M. The rear wagon was run into by engine of armoured train at level crossing on RUE DU BIEZ. The first wagon had first got over safely. The engine struck the wagon in the front. The horses were thrown on the left side, one was killed the other died later. The wagon to the right of the one. No one saw or heard the engine coming. There was no light or whistle. The driver, Dr. Atkinson was injured slightly on the head, but Sgt. Richards of the 2/R. Welsh Fusiliers, who was sitting beside him, was badly injured. He was pinned beneath the wagon injured internally. Both the	yes.

Army Form C. 2118.

WAR DIARY
or
INTELLIGENCE SUMMARY. XIX h/qrs d'Train

(Erase heading not required.)

Instructions regarding War Diaries and Intelligence Summaries are contained in F.S. Regs., Part II. and the Staff Manual respectively. Title pages will be prepared in manuscript.

Hour, Date, Place	Summary of Events and Information	Remarks and references to Appendices
ERQUINGHEM – LYS 27–5–15	Four Attivian were taken to H.Qrs. then wagon. The wagon was not to balls smashed & can be easily repaired, no worst part. Sgt. Mcnamara shell when was smashed. Pt. Kelly came to-night in relief of Lt. Whittaker who is h.Q° to 6th Div: Supply Column on position for higher rents.	/s/
28–5–15	Horses not were killed but right were buried & hoken wagon carted back to Train billet. Pt. Whittaker went to 6th div: Supply Column. 27th Division began to arrive to take over from Reg 6th.	/s/
29–5–15	Went to Railhead to Conference of Supply Officers at 3 W. Corps H.Q. Arranged to take over from 6th div: item chemicals for respirator solution. 6th Division began to leave today.	/s/
30–5–15	Officer in the kits returned - obtained chemicals for respiration from 6th div:	/s/
31–5–15	Inspected horses of all regts. & transport of 1/1 Middlesex Regt. Two bombs dropped from German aeroplane about 5 p.m. about 200 yards from side of river opp: billet, but did no damage.	

(signed) John M Amulli Major
O.C. 19th h/qrs d'Train.

(73589) W4141–463. 400,000. 9/14. H.&J.Ltd. Forms/C. 2118/10.

27TH DIVISION
19TH INFY BDE

19TH BDE TRAIN. A.S.C.
JUN-JLY 1915

12/3587

19th Brigade

19th Bde: Train

Oct XL

Army Form C. 2118.

WAR DIARY
or
INTELLIGENCE SUMMARY. XIX Inf Bde Cy Train.

(Erase heading not required.)

Instructions regarding War Diaries and Intelligence Summaries are contained in F.S. Regs., Part II. and the Staff Manual respectively. Title pages will be prepared in manuscript.

Hour, Date, Place	Summary of Events and Information	Remarks and references to Appendices
ERQUINGHEM – LYS 1-6-15	1/Middlesex Regt. took over trenches in RUE DU BOIS, previously held by 16th Inf. Bde., & No Ps. 27 to 31 inc. are weather than No 6th. Notification of this move was only received this morning, so I was able to adjust Ra. must return in time. Went to Railhead & arranged for extra Preserved meat ration.	Jas
2-6-15	Re-sent up in lieu of Frozen till further notice. No. 3 Coy. 6th Middx. Train moved on Friday this evening, but one of their horses went Lame & could not travel. I was able to Open to replace it. To Spare men one of our Spare men. Horse Lame left behind at S.O's billet & I arranged for V.O. to see it. Coy Route March in afternoon. Wheelers put up shelter for cooks, with wood provided by R.E. 1. H.D. horse to mobile Vet: Section	Jas
3-6-15	Leave of Creali renewed. Had horse left behind by 3 Coy. 6th Divis Train taken to Train Billet & treated. Company Route march in afternoon	Jas
4-6-15		Jas

WAR DIARY or INTELLIGENCE SUMMARY

Army Form C. 2118.

XIX 7 of 13th Train

Hour, Date, Place	Summary of Events and Information	Remarks and references to Appendices
ERQUINGHEM - LYS 5th - 6 - 15	Went to Railhead. Thence to 3rd Corps H.Q. to attend conference of S.S.O.s. Supply of coke afternoon had is insufficient a request was made to adm. sending more up. Off back shoring of car broke; took it to supply Colm; had news one fitted. Held musketry instruction in afternoon for all spare men.	fos.
6 - 6 - 15	1. H.D. horse shot by orders of V.O. – fractured leg. C. of E. Chaplain held gun air service for the Train at his billet in afternoon.	fos.
7 - 6 - 15	1. H.D. horse died tonight. Wagon returning into empty supply wagon. Got V.O. to examine it. He said death was due to rupture.	fos.
8 - 6 - 15.	Company Route march in afternoon.	fos.
9 - 6 - 15	6 G.S. Limbers for J.A.A. arrived today for the ammunition column. They had not sufficient drivers to take them over so sent Sgn. Beattie, Flynn, & another & transferred them here ammi. Colm-. Inoculated claim for stores taken by the troops from BOIS GRENIER.	fos.

WAR DIARY
or
INTELLIGENCE SUMMARY. XIX H/B 4 Train

(Erase heading not required.)

Army Form C. 2118.

Instructions regarding War Diaries and Intelligence Summaries are contained in F.S. Regs., Part II. and the Staff Manual respectively. Title pages will be prepared in manuscript.

Hour, Date, Place	Summary of Events and Information	Remarks and references to Appendices
ERQUINGHEM - & YS 10-6-15	Board of Officers attendance stores, ERQUINGHEM, to survey inservicable blankets. Musketry instruction made in afternoon. Gun Bearers to 19th Field Ambulance vice 8th Ses, N.B. ace tt. Requisitions received orders of supr., damaged by Armoured Train on 27 Reff, new	Inst.
11-6-15	Stationed in A.O.B. Workshops at PONT DE NIEPPE Musketry instruction parade in afternoon	Inst.
12-6-15.	Went to Railhead twice to BAILLEUL, where attacked. Conference of S.O2. Asked for load on train to be increased to 6700 min + 570 horses. F.S.C.M. Proceeding in case of J/14/6 Corpl. Bohni t whamed with asking his true N.C.O's rank was a driver of this regt. rank was driver not having evidence of cont — he reduced the rank — was inoperative while still remaining on acting Lance Corporal. Gnr Taylor Ferryman from BASE H.T. Depot.	Inst.
	(73989) W4141—463. 400,000. 9/14. H.&J.Ltd. Forms/C. 2118/10.	

WAR DIARY
or
INTELLIGENCE SUMMARY. XIX h.f.r.3 & Train

Army Form C. 2118.

(Erase heading not required.)

Instructions regarding War Diaries and Intelligence Summaries are contained in F.S. Regs., Part II and the Staff Manual respectively. Title pages will be prepared in manuscript.

Hour, Date, Place	Summary of Events and Information	Remarks and references to Appendices
ERQUINGHEM - LYS 13-6-15	Nothing to record	fras
14-6-15	Inspected horses transport opposite HQ. One roll regm vehicles rather badly. Inspected field officers A.S.C.'s & R.E. N.V.R. with view to buying grass for horses. Settled claim of M. Delebarre. Brockin for company. Route march in afternoon.	fras.
15-6-15	Inspected transport of 1/Cameronians, 1/Middlesex + 2/Royal Irish Fusiliers. all in good order. Brig. Gen. F. Gordon C.B., D.S.O. left yesterday to proceed to England to take over a Division of the new armies, & Lt. Col. P.R. Robertson C.M.G., 1/Cameronians took over command of the Brigade. Musketry instruction parade in afternoon.	
Kemmel S.	Had horses shifted from line in open field spot along hedge in accordance with orders from 27th Division. Re A.D.M.S. 27th Division inspected sanitary arrangements of the camp, more well satisfied. Park also	fras.

(73989) W4141—463. 400,000. 9/14. H.&J.Ltd. Forms/C. 2118/10.

Army Form C. 2118.

WAR DIARY
or
INTELLIGENCE SUMMARY XIX Infts de Train

(Erase heading not required.)

Instructions regarding War Diaries and Intelligence Summaries are contained in F.S. Regs., Part II. and the Staff Manual respectively. Title pages will be prepared in manuscript.

Hour, Date, Place	Summary of Events and Information	Remarks and references to Appendices
ERQUINGHEM – LYS 15-6-15.	Discovered a number of men who had objected to be inoculated & he was successful in persuading them to be done. Been looking if can leave this morning.	JOS.
16-6-15	Dr Taylor to Cleaning up, Bailleul for inspection after recovering from Enteric Fever. 14 N.C.O.s men inoculated with 1st dose. Received ink enlarged field at Bois GRENIER for Regt to cut the green grass for their horses. Arranged for Regtl. Transports to have use of forge in ERQUINGHEM in the afternoon — the gunners have them in the morning. Musketry instruction parade. Officers route march in afternoon.	JOS.
17-6-15	Went to railhead to ask for increase of forage, meet 64000 lb.	JOS.
18-6-15	To also to see if a charge could be effected with my other men. Infty Officers to get rid of some mermalade, of which we are getting 50% to 30% of Jam, to get some dried fruit instead. Musketry instruction parade in afternoon.	JOS.

(73989) W4141—463. 400,000. 9/14. H.&J.Ltd. Forms/C. 2118/10.

WAR DIARY
or
INTELLIGENCE SUMMARY. XIX Inf Bde Train.

Army Form C. 2118.

(Erase heading not required.)

Hour, Date, Place	Summary of Events and Information	Remarks and references to Appendices
ERQUINGHEM - LYS 19 - 6 - 15	Attended conference of S.S.O.s at 3rd Corps H.Q. asked for Chief Vegetables to be reduced from 18ozs lb to 9ozs lb. daily. No dried potatoes to be sent up. 27° Div: ceased to use the Lal laundry, well shirts etc. are in future to be washed by the Div: Baths. Small parts of all available men went to C. off. E. Service Min: morning at Rbt of 27th Div: from Clan. Farrier Sgt. Stembridge left this afternoon for 6 days leave of absence to England. No chloride of lime received today.	pas.
20 - 6 - 15		pas.
21 - 6 - 15	25 H.D. horses (Remounts) from 27th Div: to complete establishment. Coy: Route march in afternoon. No chloride of lime recd today.	pas.
22 - 6 - 15	Inspected kits of all M.C.O.s men to see that all were complete & also horses had not accumulated more than they could carry in event of a move. Marches in shirtsleeves in afternoon. Pte Benson proceeded to Eng'ld on 6 days leave of absence. No chloride of lime rec'd today + nb 10 gallons of creosol, smoke helmets, 1 per each officer man, received today	pas.

Army Form C. 2118.

WAR DIARY
or
INTELLIGENCE SUMMARY. XIX H/18th Train

(Erase heading not required.)

Instructions regarding War Diaries and Intelligence Summaries are contained in F.S. Regs., Part II. and the Staff Manual respectively. Title pages will be prepared in manuscript.

Hour, Date, Place	Summary of Events and Information	Remarks and references to Appendices
ERQUINGHEM - LYS 23-6-15	Accompanied G.O.C. 13th on instruction Gale 1st Lin Turnbull of Regts. also off. to Amm: Cdn. Most satisfactory. Infantry instruction parade. Capt. (Temp. Major) J.B. Ernest Dinniddie mentioned in Commander-in-Chief's despatches among others.	ps.
24-6-15	Break in the weather. Thunderclouds appeared and heavy rain fr first time for many weeks. 150 lb. Chloride of lime recd. Extra recoli. Rev: T. Brook, C.F. gave a short lecture to the men on Waterloo and had a short concert afterwards. Coy. Route March in afternoon.	ps.
25-6-15	announcement unimportant in connection with dispatches of Commander-in-Chief named today. Capt. (Temp. Major) J. Ernest Dinniddie in Le Brevet magr. dated 3/6/15. loss of recoli renewed, extra Chloride of lime recd. Infantry instruction parade in afternoon. Heavy Thunderstorm in afternoon, commencing about 3 p.m. no Chloride of lime, but recoli in lieu recd. today.	ps. ps.

(73989) W4141—463. 400,000. 9/14. H.&J.Ltd. Forms/C. 2118/10.

WAR DIARY
or
INTELLIGENCE SUMMARY XIX Inf Bde Feni

Army Form C. 2118.

(Erase heading not required.)

Hour, Date, Place	Summary of Events and Information	Remarks and references to Appendices
ERQUINGHEM – LYS 26-6-15	Visited Railhead. Hence to 3rd Corps H.Q. to conference of S.S.O.o. Asked for 4,700 eb. forges meets to be sent up on another Bn. Cons. out of trenches, on 27th Div. taking over new line. Also asked for another pack of flour. = 300 lb. will also be sent. No Chronicle of Crime but reservist rect'd in lieu holes. 48th (South Midland) Div: Leave Pari are being relieved by Canadian. 8th Div: is also transferred from 4th to 3rd Corps & is relieving 49th Div. on our right. All ranks were present. Had enquiry roll call at 9 p.m. Ferrier Sgt Stembridge returned from Leave.	JPS.
27-6-15	Divine Service for R.C.s at 11 a.m. at ERQUINGHEM Church. No Chloride flime but creosote in lieu rec'd today. Some of Lime free for men washing who asked for it. About 5 p.m. several shells were fired over & dropped on LYS sides of the river LYS behind ERQUINGHEM Church. Several of the supply details were fishing off the two Road & seven escape on 2 N.C.O.s of the R.A.M.C. who were with them, were killed & the wounded subsequently died.	JPS.

Army Form C. 2118.

WAR DIARY
or
INTELLIGENCE SUMMARY. XIX Infantry Brigade Train

(Erase heading not required.)

Instructions regarding War Diaries and Intelligence Summaries are contained in F. S. Regs., Part II. and the Staff Manual respectively. Title pages will be prepared in manuscript.

Hour, Date, Place	Summary of Events and Information	Remarks and references to Appendices
ERQUINGHEM-LYS 28-6-15	Resumption of issue of chloride of lime. Capt. Rundle March in afternoon. Drivers Granger, Edmunds, Edwards, & Hibbs arrived from B.H.T. Report. Riven draught mare - aged - with wound in	for.
29-6-15	off fore leg, strayed into our lines this evening. Stock of charcoal exhausted. Extra 6th art of trenches again. Dr. Benson returned from leave. Whilst Lt. Edgell was in the vegetable stop, paying the bill, several shells burst in the road right opposite. The car miraculously was not hit, but one man was badly wounded in the thigh. The car driver (Pte Kelly) pluckily turned his car round & picked up the wounded man & took him to the nearest Field Ambulance. 2nd (Temp. Lt.) J.A. Edgell promoted Lieut d/- 9/6/15. Musketry hakushin parade.	for.
30-6-15	G.O.C. ale inspected billets, transport lines etc. was well satisfied. No news received	for. for.

J. Cm. Mindell Major.
O.C. 19th Inf. Bde. Train.

121/6272

19th Brigade

19th Bde Train
Vol XII

WAR DIARY
or
INTELLIGENCE SUMMARY. XIX Inf. Bde. Team

(Erase heading not required.)

Army Form C. 2118.

Hour, Date, Place	Summary of Events and Information	Remarks and references to Appendices
ERQUINGHEM - LYS		
1-7-15	Rhubarb jam received for first time. No bean holes coy route march in afternoon.	fras
2-7-15	Canned maize rec'd. Extra flour & frozen meat asked for on 26th ult came up today. Raspberry & plum, strawberry & plum jam received for first time. No bean breakfast tomorrow parade.	fras
3-7-15	Went to Railhead. Men & 3 Corps HQ were attended conference Offrs. O/CM Brigade left for England on leave. No bean again today, but canned maize instead. This is 2nd july also.	frst
4-7-15	Bran received, and no maize. No Bacon, but M.V. Ration in lieu. Jennie for C. of E. at 10.30 a.m. at LIERINETTE; Lt. Miller marched men. Special leave train started today, leaving STEENWERCK at 4.30 p.m.	fras

WAR DIARY
or
INTELLIGENCE SUMMARY. XIX A.f.A & Train

(Erase heading not required.)

Army Form C. 2118.

Instructions regarding War Diaries and Intelligence Summaries are contained in F.S. Regs., Part II. and the Staff Manual respectively. Title pages will be prepared in manuscript.

Hour, Date, Place	Summary of Events and Information	Remarks and references to Appendices
ERQUINGHEM - LYS 5-7-15	2/o Bacon, Lieut M.N. Return in lieu. Conform orde march in afternoon under Lt Pakenham. Lecture at 12 noon at 27th Div. H.Q. to Capt. J. Bailey on method of preservation & spraying of smoke helmets	pas.
6-7-15	Musketry instruction parade in afternoon. Sgt Egle left for leave in Ireland	
7-7-15	Auction issued. Rest arrived at Railhead in hanleted truck. Musketry instruction parade in afternoon. Inspected transport of 19th Field Ambulance found everything satisfactory	pas.
8-7-15	Visited Railhead made inquiries re obtaining of Rick Salt & linseed especially looked him Ofpehol. D.D. of S.T. II Army had advised rat letter tea to arrive today but it did not come up. The proformer have been asked for for some time have not yet arrived. Route march in afternoon. It. Hone climbered in H. It prahel. Gift apples received for distribution in Brigade	pas.

WAR DIARY
or
INTELLIGENCE SUMMARY XIX Inf. of 13th Train

Army Form C. 2118.

(Erase heading not required.)

Hour, Date, Place	Summary of Events and Information	Remarks and references to Appendices
ERQUINGHEM – LYS 9-7-15	Inspected all horses of Hqrs & Amm. Coln. with particular attention to min shoeing; raced on the whole is very good. Musketry Instruction parade in afternoon. 2/Cpl. Turyton returned from leave.	pas
10-7-15	S. Sgt. Crook left for leave in England. Went to conference of S.S. O. at 3rd Corps H.Q. Asked for each Division once a week & Lack of truck salt 3 times a week. Filter sent up on Am Train. About 6 German shells sent over ERQUINGHEM this afternoon but they did no damage.	pas
11-7-15	Capt. P. Prospet, Interpreter, left this afternoon for leave. C. of E service for some men this morning at billets of pris. From Clan. Inspected transport of 13th Amm. Coln; very satisfactory. Dr. Edmunds 13th Dr. H.Q. in Nherof. Dr. Dickson temporarily in H. D. Have transferred to Canals Clearing Hosp. BAILLEUL	pas

Army Form C. 2118.

WAR DIARY
or
INTELLIGENCE SUMMARY. XIX Inf. B. & T rain

(Erase heading not required.)

Instructions regarding War Diaries and Intelligence Summaries are contained in F. S. Regs., Part II. and the Staff Manual respectively. Title pages will be prepared in manuscript.

Hour, Date, Place	Summary of Events and Information	Remarks and references to Appendices
ERQUINGHEM – LYS 12-7-15	Company route march in afternoon	JBS
13-7-15	Sgt Eyle returned from leave. A small quantity of mutton rec.d lately. Smoke helmets inspected & reshaped where necessary by Respirator Officer Lt Ford R.A.M.C. Pte Vies detained in H.	
14-7-15	1 Riding horse to Mobile Veterinary Section. Received orders tonight for Train to move to new billet about ¾ mile S. of STEENWERCK. Sack of Rock salt & no. of binned arrived rations for 1st Div. weekly issue to be made in future.	JBS
15-7-15	Train moved to new billets about ¾ mile S. of STEENWERCK. Supply Sect remained behind at ERQUINGHEM.	JBS
STEENWERCK 16-7-15	Arranged for 1st Line transport to take rations into trenches & Revn allow empty wagons to return to their billet early, as otherwise they would not get back till after midnight.	JBS

(73989) W4141—463. 400,000. 9/14. H.&J.Ltd. Forms/C. 2118/10.

WAR DIARY
or
INTELLIGENCE SUMMARY. XIX H.Q. of Train

Army Form C. 2118.

(Erase heading not required.)

Instructions regarding War Diaries and Intelligence Summaries are contained in F.S. Regs., Part II and the Staff Manual respectively. Title pages will be prepared in manuscript.

Hour, Date, Place	Summary of Events and Information	Remarks and references to Appendices
STEENWERCK 16-7-15	S/Sgt. Cook returned from leave. Meat ration reduced to 1 lb. frozen & (nominal) preserved + condensed milk issued – when available – at rate of 6 rations to a tin.	
17-7-15	Int's Conference of S.O.'s at 3rd Corps H.Q. Brig: Gen. A.Q. = Chichester has taken over Dr. A.D.M.S. from Brig: Gen. L. Campbell. SM.A.3 Det moved to new billets beside Train Coy billet. Condensed milk received again today. Rum issue to hosps in trenches knighthoused by G.O.C. Refilling point changed to Road Junction ½ mile N.W. of CROIX DU BAC. Settled claim of Mons Matelin for use of chaff-cutter at ERQUINGHEM what B's were billeted. Pre	ffs.
18-7-15	Dr. Graeme to 19th Field Ambulance. 1 H.D. horse to B de H.Q. 2nd Lieut Harris proceeded on leave to England. Condensed milk acc. loan of horse June in addition to fresh requisition. Dr. I've from H.Q. i Dr. Tayler to H.Q. + sent to Base saw O.C. 8th Div: Train + the S.S.O., as we are shortly to be attached to the 8th Div:. on leaving No 27?. B'de relieved tonight + moved to billets W. + N.W. of STEENWERCK. Refuge wagon sent to units first thing.	ffs.
19-7-15		

Forms/C. 2118/10.

WAR DIARY
or
INTELLIGENCE SUMMARY. XIX Bgde Train

(Erase heading not required.)

Army Form C. 2118.

Hour, Date, Place	Summary of Events and Information	Remarks and references to Appendices
STEENWERCK 19-7-15	morning. after refilling Supply wagons returned to train filled & went to Rev Regts. in evening after Rev arrived in new billets. Condensed milk rec⁴	
20-7-15	B⁸ᵉ attached to 8ᵗʰ Brigade: from 12 noon today after refilling Supply wagons returned to train filled & went up to units in afternoon. 1 case of Red Currant jam.	JBS.
21-7-15	Major S/O Conducting Middle issued on leave to England. Batapukta Parapet admin S.M. STEENWERCK Supply of Condensed milk stopped. Veterinary Officer ordered horse with fractured leg to be shot, which was done. Visited S.A.D. 8ᵗʰ Bn. re coal. This to be drawn from Sailly. Orders Recd orders to move tomorrow afternoon.	JBS. OS
22-7-15 Doulieu	Reveille early and moved all Supply wagons to railway at once. As ordered applied to O.C. 8ᵗʰ Divⁿ Train for allotment of billets. Fixed on a field at SDOULIEN First half of Train moved off after lunch for new billets to prepare horselines &c. Remainder followed when loaded. Supply details billeted at Nouveau Monde. Inspected Supply Column Officers of position of Church in Church at Nouveau Monde. Reported new billets to 19ᵗʰ Bgde HQ and also wired same to DB of S&T.	OS

Army Form C. 2118.

WAR DIARY
or
INTELLIGENCE SUMMARY. XIX Inf Bde of Trui

(Erase heading not required.)

Instructions regarding War Diaries and Intelligence Summaries are contained in F.S. Regs., Part II and the Staff Manual respectively. Title pages will be prepared in manuscript.

Hour, Date, Place	Summary of Events and Information	Remarks and references to Appendices
DOULIEU 23.7.15	Refilled at position midway Sailly-Estaires. Baggage wagons sent to units. 5 whole horse returned from furlough. Mr Mahar proceeded on furlough. Supply wagons after refilling were parked in Church square to await arrival of their respective units who moved into position LAVENTIE Trenches. 89 Sabine Buckets for units lacking own turned this evening.	A.D
24.7.15	An examination of 8th Dt Ro 647, all records &limits were marked with date of issue. an inspection made and certificate rendered to Brig. H.Q. Certificate rendered that no officer or man in this unit was qualified or certified quality as interpreter in Incharch or Guide. Attended Conference of Supply officers at Bailleul. It has been decided that in England by the authorities that maize be sent up on draws. Vegetables cannot be obtained in bulk from Dunkirk. When MTV is based in lieu of Bacon no condensed milk to be issued Render report on Bread (Biscuit ration as to wastage + out of ration	A.D
25.7.15	Rifle Inspection. Names — sent of men wishing to retain Service periods of war (A.R 13/4 (22 of June.))	A.D
26.7.15	Car was run into this morning by Highland Div Ambulance and had injured. No blame attaches to our Chauffeur. Supply Column to draw Rations from Thiennes for three days. The Brigade Taken of by O/C 5th Scottish Rifles Similarly quantity of Strawberry Jam up.	A.D

(73989) W4141—463. 400,000. 9/14. H.&J.Ltd. Forms/C. 2118/10.

WAR DIARY
or
INTELLIGENCE SUMMARY XIX Inf. Bde. 13th Train

(Erase heading not required.)

Army Form C. 2118.

Instructions regarding War Diaries and Intelligence Summaries are contained in F.S. Regs., Part II and the Staff Manual respectively. Title pages will be prepared in manuscript.

Hour, Date, Place	Summary of Events and Information	Remarks and references to Appendices
DOULIEU		
27.7.15	Licensed & Rock perl issued. Lt. Pakenham sent to Ammunition Column in order to relieve Capt. Block proceeding on leave. A Br'y's inspected horses of Train.	as
28.7.15	Lt. Edgell doing Transport Duties. Great difficulty in obtaining Orders Coke wood issued in lieu. 1 LD & 1 HD horse to No 15 mobile vet Section	as
29.7.15	Major Polland-Brindelli returned from leave last night. Capt. Graham proceeded to England on leave. Bought 6 tons of coal on new available at milherd	Jas.
30.7.15	Visited railhead, now LA GORGUE. Inspection of traces helmets. Gift tinned salmon received.	Jas.
31.7.15	Ferrier Capt. Potter to B.A. HQ. endeavouring to look after horses Rev. whilst so far away from Train billet. Pte Prince admitted to HP. Attended conference of S.O.o at 3rd Corps HQ. Discussed plan of light railways for conveying return stores from railway to trenches	Jas.

John McCullin Major
O.C. 19th Inf. B.de Train

(Became No. 2 Coy. 2nd
Divisional Train 19.8.15)

19th INFANTRY BRIGADE TRAIN.

A U G U S T

1 9 1 5

(1.8.15-19.8.15)

Army Form C. 2118.

WAR DIARY
or
INTELLIGENCE SUMMARY. XIX Inf Bde Train

(Erase heading not required.)

Instructions regarding War Diaries and Intelligence Summaries are contained in F.S. Regs., Part II and the Staff Manual respectively. Title pages will be prepared in manuscript.

Hour, Date, Place	Summary of Events and Information	Remarks and references to Appendices
DOULIEU, FRANCE 1-8-15	Visited railhead at La GORGUE. Bought 40 hectolitres of coke from MERVILLE granaries. One lorry is in use at Railhead. 1 L.D. horse to mobile veterinary section.	ffs.
2-8-15	Mr. Dixon proceeded on leave to England. 1 case of Raspberry Jam.	ffs
3-8-15	Inspected transport of 5th Cameron Rifles, 2/R. Welsh Fusiliers, o/2nd A.T.H. Two 13th & 18th H.P. of 59 Inf Bde (20 & 2nd Bn.) are attached to min Bde for instruction. Supplies to be supervised by mB S.O.	ffs.
4-8-15	Smoke helmets inspected by Bde Reqn Officer & Bdes Rolld up. It pours stopped. Went to Forêt de Nieppe to try to get hot hole for Bde signalling officer. Was unsuccessful. Reg must be obtained through RE.	ffs.
5-8-15	New system of issue of Bread Meat. Have arrived at Railhead today, but will arrive early tomorrow morning when Reg Supply column	ffs.

(73989) W4141—463. 400,000. 9/14. H.&J.Ltd. Forms/C. 2118/10.

Army Form C. 2118.

WAR DIARY
or
INTELLIGENCE SUMMARY. XIX 2f/13 a Train

(Erase heading not required.)

Instructions regarding War Diaries and Intelligence Summaries are contained in F. S. Regs., Part II. and the Staff Manual respectively. Title pages will be prepared in manuscript.

Hour, Date, Place	Summary of Events and Information	Remarks and references to Appendices
DOULIEU 5-8-15	Took up stores to Refilling Point. This saved as usual with rest of supplies for consumption on the following day. Truck of Coal & coke sent to Railhead for this R.C., were emptied by Supply Column with empty head meet train. Went to H.Q. from 'A.D. of S.' in accordance with orders received from him, & communicated to him position of Refilling Point & Billets of Supply Column.	
6-8-15	Designation of unit to which it belongs, painted on "dead" of Cars in accordance with Army Orders. Sgt Walker to Base Hospital - kicked by horse. Pte Ferguson 619 Field Ambulance temporarily	Yes Yes
7-8-15	Visited Railhead. Condensed milk arrived today for issue tomorrow. Went to 3rd Corps H.Q. attended Conference of S.O.O. Capt. W.J. Danbury, O.C. J.H.Q.3 Column, proceeded to England on leave. Lt. Pakenham returned for duty on return of Capt.	Yes

Army Form C. 2118.

WAR DIARY
or
INTELLIGENCE SUMMARY. XIX Inf/Bde Train
(Erase heading not required.)

Instructions regarding War Diaries and Intelligence Summaries are contained in F.S. Regs., Part II. and the Staff Manual respectively. Title pages will be prepared in manuscript.

Hour, Date, Place	Summary of Events and Information	Remarks and references to Appendices
DOULIEU 7-8-15	Flint from leave. Capt. Birkenshaw, S.O., went to live at Refilling Point. Dr Bailey admitted to FP.	Yes.
8-6-15	1 H.D. have to Mobile Veterinary Section, obtained donkies	Yes.
9-8-15	Blanket vehicles returned from unit. 1 G.S. wagon complete turn out (8 horses) sent to G.O.C. R.A. 20th Div.; 3 G.S. wagon complete turn out — (from Liskar, Gilkes, & Barleem) sent to 8 Gun Redoubt & Hartfield with 2 civilian carts (blankets) rec'd from 19th Field Ambulance. Raw + 7 men. 1 D.V.H. + 1 other admitted to FP	Yes.
10-8-15	Capt. Birkenshaw proceeded on leave to England. Lt. Edgell has taken over supply duties during his absence & went to live at Refilling Point. Cheese ration reduced to 3/4 oz:	Yes.
11-8-15	2 H.D. + 1 Riding horse to 1/Middlesex Regt.; 3 H.D. horses to 5 Scottish Rifles; 1 H.D. horse to 2/R Irish Fusiliers; 1 H.D. horse to 2 Comp. Div.; 1 H.D. horse to 19th Field Ambulance. Company Sports took place this afternoon.	Yes.

(73989) W4141—463. 400,000. 9/14. H.&J.Ltd. Forms/C. 2118/10.

WAR DIARY
or
INTELLIGENCE SUMMARY. XIX h.f. 13th Train

(Erase heading not required.)

Army Form C. 2118.

Instructions regarding War Diaries and Intelligence Summaries are contained in F. S. Regs., Part II. and the Staff Manual respectively. Title pages will be prepared in manuscript.

Hour, Date, Place	Summary of Events and Information	Remarks and references to Appendices
DOULIEU 12-8-15	Visited Railhead. Dr McClellan & Dr Bailey discharged from H.	
13-8-15	Dr Knight & one horse with forge (blanket) cast back from 19th Field Ambulance. Inspected Transport/Camerons found many minor repairs reqd. & harness	/or.
14-8-15	Visited Railhead. Also went to 3rd Corps H.Q. Which is now at LA MOTTE, to Conference of S.S.O.s. Was informed that an extra 1lb. of fresh vegetables was sanctioned in lieu of evaporation too as reduction of cheese ration; also that rice was allowed to be drawn in lieu of biscuit or bread. Got Brig: Horse shoers. Entered 3 guns with waggon, 1 pitchforks, Heavy draught (b) Long Reins (8) R & D. Too B 3rd large bath 2 Ladles. Also entered for best Mounted N.C.O., Cyclist, Means & Light draught horse in show, but was not successful in any.	/or. /or.

Army Form C. 2118.

WAR DIARY
or
INTELLIGENCE SUMMARY. XIX Inf. Bde. Train

(Erase heading not required.)

Instructions regarding War Diaries and Intelligence
Summaries are contained in F.S. Regs., Part II.
and the Staff Manual respectively. Title pages
will be prepared in manuscript.

Hour, Date, Place	Summary of Events and Information	Remarks and references to Appendices
DOULIEU 15-8-15	½ of the Bn. was relieved tonight & marched into billets between DOULIEU & NEUF BERQUIN. They had their Baggage wagon. Remainder has had own Res Baggage supply wagon, & had each took a load of stores back. Supply wagon, after refilling, & these units returned to Train billet & went up to their units in evening. Lt Edgell Supply Off. returned to billets of Train this afternoon. Recd. instruction that Bn to to go to 2nd Division shortly. Went in 1st Army H.Q. to see officer to arrange about move & to arrange about supplies.	
16-8-15	Remainder of Bn was relieved tonight & marched to billets near Ohero. Bn Hd. H.Q. moved to LE VERRIER. Supply wagon Refilling Point changed to road junction on ESTAIRES – DOULIEU road 1½ miles S. of DOULIEU. Supply wagon went to mils direct. Baggage wagons for units moved today, have sent to units this afternoon. Both baggage supply wagon moved a load of stores back, from old to new billets. Yesterday afternoon. Went to II Division area and saw O.C. Train & S.S.O. ee on	Ys.

(73989) W4141—463. 400,000. 9/14. H.&J.Ltd. Forms/C. 2118/10.

Army Form C. 2118.

WAR DIARY
or
INTELLIGENCE SUMMARY. XIX ~ h/f B 2 Train

(Erase heading not required.)

Hour, Date, Place	Summary of Events and Information	Remarks and references to Appendices
DOULIEU 16-8-15	Move to be merged into No II Div: Train in to place of No Guards B. Co:. Lt. Edmonds to Paris H.	
17-8-15	Visited units made arrangements for move on 19 inst. Wired S.S.O. II Div: ration & stores knowing consumption on 20 ct. Capt. Pakenham returned from leave. Lt. Pakenham & Capt. Luke proceeded to England on leave. Lt. Packard & Supplys wagon returned to R.A. Ammunition Column, were leave no Brigade Ammun + march & Advanced Base H.T. Depot.	yes.
18-8-15	Supply Column, after dumping rations this morning for consumption tomorrow, left for R.H.Q. to form nucleus of Guards Div: Supplys Column. Wired S.S.O. II Div: ration to be drawn tomorrow for consumption or 21st. H.D. Wace to mobile Veterinary Section, bed kick on able to haul.	yes.
19-8-15	Train left billet at 8.15 p.m. & marched to new billet at BETHUNE & joined II Division. Baggage wagons which had been sent to units back yesterday were assembled & proceeded & proceeded join the Train to rente. Supply section, empty of supplies, carried surplus	

(73989) W4141—463. 400,000. 9/14. H.&J.Ltd. Forms/C. 2118/10.

WAR DIARY
or
INTELLIGENCE SUMMARY. XIX Inf. Bde Train

Army Form C. 2118.

(Erase heading not required.)

Hour, Date, Place	Summary of Events and Information	Remarks and references to Appendices
DOULIEU 19-8-15	Hauled other stores of units dumped from at Train's rear billet & then proceeded to refilling point in BETHUNE. Refilled at 3 P.M.; MOR supplies to units & then returned to Train billet. Train caught up 10th 1¾ miles N. of HINGES at 11.45 P.M. Here watered + fed + marched off at 1.15 P.M. in rear of M Bty. Lost kitchen on M Bty march past adjust S. of HINGES. Own billet reached at 2 P.M. 19th Bn Train cease to exist & M Coys now becomes Divisional Train. Dr Angus admitted to IF.	

John Morris Lieut Major
O.C. 19th Inf. B. Q. Train

RESERVE BRIGADE TRAIN

OCTOBER & NOVEMBER 1914.

121/2590

Ulster Brigade Train

Vol I.   14.10 — 30.11.14

WAR DIARY

Period. (a) 14 October to 31st October
1914.
(b) 1st November to 30th November.

From.

Captain G. Fraser Maclean.
O.C. Reserve Brigade
Train.

G.H.Q

Army Form C. 2118.

WAR DIARY
or
INTELLIGENCE SUMMARY.
(Erase heading not required.)

Instructions regarding War Diaries and Intelligence Summaries are contained in F.S. Regs., Part II. and the Staff Manual respectively. Title pages will be prepared in manuscript.

Hour, Date, Place	Summary of Events and Information	Remarks and references to Appendices
14 October 15/14/1914 LE BOISLE. 7 P.M.	Left at Lt STONER, with 14 Wagons Oats & 14 Lorries loaded with Oats, by order of D.S.T. S.4 h.Q – Arrived and reported at D.S.T. Office. STONER Lorries & Wagons parked in Infantry Barracks.	
October 15th "	Lt CROKER. A.S.C. reported arrival, as Supply Officer to No 1 Location Reserve Ricapple Train. Took over 1st & 2nd of 26 Coy A.S.C. and 3 Horses. From Captain Prescott Roberts A.S.C. Oats in Wagons and Lorries, Lorries over and handed over to S. Officer G.H.Q. Received instructions from D.S.T. G.H.Q. regarding formation of Reserve Parks. Despatched to Drivers, under Sgt HORLOCK, A.S.C. to purchase Saddlery purchased horses – 16 Horses returned. Received from Field Cashier G.H.Q. 2000 francs. Imprest account.	
October 16th "	Received 5 Country Carts from Of. i/c E – Reserve Parks for Parcels without Turnouts Open – Unable to take over Supply Column Officers. Despatched 12 Drivers under Sgt HORLOCK. to BREMES, n Calais R! to bring back purchased Horses – forwarded demands to Ordnance D.W.S Base for Drivers –	
October 17th "		

WAR DIARY
or
INTELLIGENCE SUMMARY.

(Erase heading not required.)

Army Form C. 2118.

Instructions regarding War Diaries and Intelligence Summaries are contained in F. S. Regs., Part II. and the Staff Manual respectively. Title pages will be prepared in manuscript.

Hour, Date, Place	Summary of Events and Information	Remarks and references to Appendices
October 18th 1914 ST OMER.	2 French Carts received from O.T. II Reserve Park. 16 Horses despatched to O.T. II Reserve Park at ANVIN — under Corporal RIDEON, also 11 B.S. Wagons — 22 Horses under Sgt GOULD, A.S.C. with instructions to report to O.C. 2. Reserve Park —	✓
October 19th "	Sent 8 drivers — who reported for 2. Reserve Park, who returning 16 ANVIN. Detained 6 B.S. Wagons 17 Horses (drivers from NANTES) & brought them up to Strength. Remainder ST OMER. Paid Detachment 270 francs. Took over 2 Horses from D.D.R.G.H.Q. —	Eden.
Thurs 20th "	8 B.S. Wagons — complete worked over 6 (?steep) Battery Artillery People with Drivers — under Dy Sgt T. L. All Horses inspected by V.O. 9AM. Handed over one County Cart - to S. Irish Horse. — Obtained Receipt. Purchased Cart. In process of repairs. Harness in very bad state. Reported Ca.	Reference Vehicle Repair " Eden

Army Form C. 2118.

WAR DIARY
or
INTELLIGENCE SUMMARY.
(Erase heading not required.)

Instructions regarding War Diaries and Intelligence Summaries are contained in F.S. Regs., Part II. and the Staff Manual respectively. Title pages will be prepared in manuscript.

Hour, Date, Place	Summary of Events and Information	Remarks and references to Appendices
October 21st 1914. ST OMER.	Detachment Convoy in charge of 1st Portion at Rly Station & hence to Billets. Dad Captn Rothstede reported (Read by Coy into the Barrack in duty. Detachment employed on general duties.	
October 22nd "	Proceeded to HAZEBROUCK — reported also CAESTRE by order of D.A.D.T. to see R.T.O. and Officer Commanding Ammunition Column. reported. Bivouac FOREW Union	
October 23rd	Discharged 70 horses at ROUEN via STOMER & despatched 3S to D.I. N° 1. Reserve Park. 2S TO D. N° 11. " " " by order of D.A.D.T. Stores. Took over on horse from Madame MORELL. ST OMER. from in relation of D.D.R.G./H.R. Paid the sum of 18 francs a-c (12 days) in keep of horses. Left by 4th Divisional Train. — Detachment employed on Remount duties, & local Transport work —	Receipts represented to OCTRem/14

Army Form C. 2118.

WAR DIARY
or
INTELLIGENCE SUMMARY.
(Erase heading not required.)

Instructions regarding War Diaries and Intelligence Summaries are contained in F. S. Regs., Part II. and the Staff Manual respectively. Title pages will be prepared in manuscript.

Hour, Date, Place	Summary of Events and Information	Remarks and references to Appendices
October 24th/1914. STONER.	Distributed 32 Wagons - 64 Horses - 32 Drivers - Per Station STONER. 1 Wagon per 1st Divl. [Divisional] Artillery Brigade. 7 2 Wagons 1st Div: Artillery Brigade. } report to 1st Divn 2 Wagons, G.S. Park. " " } Artillery Brigade H.Q.s The above were despatched under Corporal RIDGE on one. to STAPLES _ for night; proceeding in morning to BAILLEUL.	Signed
October 25th	24 Wagons - distributed as follows by order of A.D.V.S. 4th Divn. 12 Wagons. Dvl. 2. Reserve Park. 12 " " Dvl. 5. " " Dvl. 6. " " The above were taken over by Captain English ASC.	Per Vehicle Persoy Signed
October 26th	2 G.S. Wagons sent to SETQUES. to report to OC. 6th Reserve Park by order of A.D.V.S. Detachment employed on General duties.	Signed

Army Form C. 2118.

WAR DIARY
or
INTELLIGENCE SUMMARY.
(Erase heading not required.)

Instructions regarding War Diaries and Intelligence Summaries are contained in F.S. Regs., Part II. and the Staff Manual respectively. Title pages will be prepared in manuscript.

Hour, Date, Place	Summary of Events and Information	Remarks and references to Appendices
Oct. 27th 1914 ST OMER	1 S.S. Wagon - Complete to 1st Corps Artillery Brigade Hd Qrs YPRES. by new 4 Ton Lorry attd. 2/Lt DOWSE A.S.C. reported in chg of the Reserve Supply Park Train. Inspected Transport of Royal Irish Regt - in possession 13 Officers Horses - 3 Cart.	
Oct. 28th	Inspected Transport. D.O.O(Instructional) Horses, Harness, Harness, – report sent in to D.A.D.T. G.H.Q. Inspected Transport. LONDON SCOTTISH. Vehicles inspected. Reserve horse vehicle shoes - sent Farrier to help - & olive Horner. This Bge required 2 G.S.wagons for blankets. Two Inspects Waterers sent & receipt obtained. Detachment employed in General duties.	30/10/14."

WAR DIARY
or
INTELLIGENCE SUMMARY.
(*Erase heading not required.*)

Army Form C. 2118.

Hour, Date, Place	Summary of Events and Information	Remarks and references to Appendices
October 25th ST OMER.	Inspected Transport of ARTIST. Rifles. T. — Vehicles in good condition, a few minor repairs required to Limber Wagons, adjuster in wheeler shop — This Corps had no cold Shoes — One applied for. Sent 2 GS Wagons, complete to H.Q. 3rd Corps. BAILLEUL. Morning, to to CHOQUES Ry Station the following morning with 1 Wagon — for 114th Siege Battery, to be called for by a Representative — 1 GS Wagon for 115 Battery — to be called for at BAILLEUL. hydra 9 & 9 T — S.A.A. —	Ecm
October 30th and 31st Oct'br. ST OMER.	went to BAILLEUL, to find out expected wagons — 114 Bat'y as no representative called — arranged to Return. wit. S. opric BAILLEUL — also proceeded to CHOQUES, and arranged to Return etc — for wagon — left there. 2 wagons — empty, taken over by Raid'n Div A.M.T. depot. I brought to Orfnks howls. gales 9 9 of — Officers on horse [or] Jt. DOWSE ate. attached to D.R. PMO. Lieut. received in Errard Inshin.	army Foi

WAR DIARY or INTELLIGENCE SUMMARY.

Army Form C. 2118.

(Erase heading not required.)

Hour, Date, Place	Summary of Events and Information	Remarks and references to Appendices
1.11.14: ST OMER.	Detachment employed in General duties, Rations & General work. Made arrangements to have all horses belonging to 2 M Royal Irish Reg. Shod on the expired shoes, lastly. Established a Farriers shop in Depots Remits.	Sgn
2.11.14	20 S.S. Wagons, 39 Horses, 19 Drivers arrived at H.Q. 8 from LE MANS. H.T. Depot. In distribution to Units. 1st PARK Transport belongs to Horse Artillery Brig. All vehicles in good Condition. Horses & Harness to Horse Artillery Brig. All Horses in fair repair, 1st Reserve Horses required Shoeing. Deficient of 1 Cable wagon. Sent 4 wagons empties DE TRANSFIE(L)D to report to O.C. 7 Reserve Park at FAUQUEMBERGUES in need of HORSES at HAZEBR.LIS. receipt obtained.	Sgn
3.11.14	Handed over to 2 M R. Irish Reg. Horse shoeing Transport from H.Q. T. Depot LE MANS. 2 Water Carts— complete. 2 S.S. Wagons. 1 Rolling Cart 4 S.S. Wagons 3 Trains 6 S.A.A. Carts. 2 limbered S.S. Wagons. Total Horses 23 L. Draft. 12 Heavy Draft. 9 Drivers out Drivers for Reserve P&c Transport from base 1 WOLSELEY Ambulance, handed over to M.C. O.C. 4th Reserve Park Mob. T.O. ARTIST RIFLES — 1 S.A.A. Cart, 1 Cabinet wagon, 2 Blanket Wagon. Complete. Received from H.T. Depot LE MANS Complete Transport of 7. Section Depot Coy. at LONGENESSE.	Receipt ✓
		Sgn

Army Form C. 2118.

WAR DIARY
or
INTELLIGENCE SUMMARY.
(Erase heading not required.)

Instructions regarding War Diaries and Intelligence Summaries are contained in F.S. Regs., Part II. and the Staff Manual respectively. Title pages will be prepared in manuscript.

Hour, Date, Place	Summary of Events and Information	Remarks and references to Appendices
4.11.14 - St OMER.	Detachment on General Duties - & local works - Deputated 4 B.S. Waggons in charge of Cpl Rose & one to St JANS CAPPEL for Q.O.O.R. of Wm. Hussars. 1 G.S. Wagon sent to D.C. LAHORE - Reserve Park and a limbered waggon exchanged, 4 extra of Dep. T. Stores - Heavy Wagon despatched 4 picks to OC. H.T. Depot RUEN. Inspected Transport of ROYAL HIGHLANDERS and report sent in to D/f.T. also ROYAL WARWICKSHIRE Regt R.H.A. 4 officers + 134 A Gart - returned by LONDON SCOTTISH as not wanted 9 Horses, 4 drivers ASC + 1/2 Corporal. 1 Horse left sick - at HAZEBROUCK. also 1 Horse left of ARTIST RIFLES at HELFAUT. reported to D.D.V.S.	[illegible notes]
5.11.14.	Handed over to 2 Royal IRISH Regt. 24 Cookers, by order of D/f. S.T.O. - Receipt Taken. Transport of Queen Westminster Rifles, T. inspected. A good order - mostly all civilian lorries. Some very light + small - also inspected. Devonshire Yeomany complete - about 3 Civilian waggons rather heavy for Cavalry work - remarks all government Transport. reported D/DT. S.T.O.	[illegible]
6.11.14.	Inspected Transport 10, SCOTTISH LIVERPOOL Regt. Vehicles in good order. a number of civilian lorries - Dozer Cart - Mess Tipts - This Battalion had no Carts shown - Indicated T.O. to apply also Replant has roller & the Officer (name) and truck to the Horses & Troopers - Regmtl. Horses Reported Passing. [illegible]	[illegible]

Army Form C. 2118.

WAR DIARY
or
INTELLIGENCE SUMMARY.
(Erase heading not required.)

Instructions regarding War Diaries and Intelligence Summaries are contained in F. S. Regs., Part II. and the Staff Manual respectively. Title pages will be prepared in manuscript.

Hour, Date, Place	Summary of Events and Information	Remarks and references to Appendices
7.11.14. STOMER.	Two G.S. Wagons despatched to ARQUES, taking in ammunition under escort to Infantry Barracks STOMER. In Territorial Brigade. Despatched under 3 D/St. S.B.S. Wagons — 1 Parcel Cart to HAZEBROUCK, en route to BAILLEUL, to Q.Q. Ordshire Stewart — also one French Cart to Hd. of S.E. Div. Hd Qs R.E. — And one French Cart to 5₂ Co/R.E. at SAILLY — receipt obtained.	[signature]
8.11.14.	Inspected Transport 1st + 2nd line of 8th Bn Royal SCOTS - T. of NEWRINGHAM. All Vehicles in good order — required one pole also some minor repairs. Sent saddler also Farrier to help. Inspected G.H.L. Infantry — at WARDREQUES — Vehicles all G.S. Wagons, with exception of T.M.A. Carts which were light 4 wheeled curtain wagons. This the weakin harness of 2 G.S. drivers — Their Pertebem had plenty of Tools & horse shoes — 1 G.S. wagon despatched to 5. SCOTTISH Rifles, to replace broken one — Temporarily wagon brought in for repair.	[signature]
9.11.14.	Detached expired on leave Transport work. Barttn of MONMOUTH & ANGLESEA R.E. Inspected Transport of 1st HERTFORDSHIRE Regt. — This Batallin had 2 Cookers — Private property — Transfers — also Vehicles — mostly civilian wagons in good condition, but required minor repairs — 1 broken pole replaced — one wagon left at Ry station — repaired & returned.	[signature]

WAR DIARY
INTELLIGENCE SUMMARY
(Erase heading not required.)

Army Form C. 2118.

Hour, Date, Place	Summary of Events and Information	Remarks and references to Appendices
10.11.14. ST. OMER	Sent 2 French Carts to Indian Corps. Enroute with R.E. Detachment. Replaced in Divnal. Supply Transport by 4 F.W.D. Royal Irish Fusiliers. Vehicles in good order. 6 S.A.A. all Divns. & French Wagons + Horses required shoeing - also Reim Repairs - One G.S. Wagon required Pole Pin, also Pole Carriage required adjustment. Palestine Troopers in various stables. Sent 1 G.M.R. Cart to Seaforth Scottish Rifles – being short of one. Also several repairs carried out to Vehicles. Received 18 following Transport (Mules) from HQ 3rd Division. Horses 25. G.S. Wagons 7. Limbered Wagons 2. Israel Carts 4. 1 S.H.A. Cart. 1 Water Cart. Vehicles in bad condition also Harness & Horses very poor condition. Polled & required rest. Inspected by V.O. S.H.A. Mainly Drivers, with Transport - Viz U. Middlesex Regt. 1 Royal Scots. 9. Inns. Argyll Reg. 4 A.S.C. Drivers.	Epm Epm
11.11.14. ST. OMER	1 French Cart, sent by order of D.y.G. to 9 Stationary Mobile Section at HAZEBROUCK. 1 French Cart to O.C. No. G.R.E. ESTAIRES. 1 French Cart to O.C. 3 Coy. R.E. at LOCON – receipt obtained – Inspected Transport of N. Somerset Yeomanry – all Vehicles & Harness in Good Condition – Replaced one Cart in 2 Monmouth Regt. unserviceable. Imported Transport with adjutant	Vehicles Repairs. Epm

Army Form C. 2118.

WAR DIARY
or
INTELLIGENCE SUMMARY.
(Erase heading not required.)

Instructions regarding War Diaries and Intelligence Summaries are contained in F.S. Regs., Part II. and the Staff Manual respectively. Title pages will be prepared in manuscript.

Hour, Date, Place	Summary of Events and Information	Remarks and references to Appendices
11.11.14. ST OMER. (contd)	90 Horses arrived for Remounts for Reserve Parks – handed over to 2/Lt RICHARDSON – I/c dety of DPT – to BETQUES. Detachment returned on completion.	
12.11.14.	Inspected Transport S.S. ZENON Regt – Wagons in good order, harness required minor repairs – harness rag mixed – practically territorial units but harness which was patched up – several Austrian Collars required repairs, Shoeing not good. 20 Wagons, 40 Horses, 20 Drivers, taken off Rail from M.T. Depot LE MANS. Capt LUSAS in Charge – went on to Supp. 6 Reserve Park at BETQUES.	Ellis
13.11.14.	20 Heavy Wagons, complete pleased on Rail to M.T. Depot HAVRE, 60 Horses – 60 Horses arrived from Remounts – Havre – & handed over to OWEN are No 3. R. Park.	Ellis
14.11.14	Inspected Transport 6th CHESHIRE Regt – 26 Carts 2 Cookers Wagons, 2 Cookers, Heavy Wagon. Remainder S.S. Wagons in good condition – Several Carts of harness required adjustment – Collars in poor condition – Harness required shoeing intricate To be clerical equipment required, also tire obsolete, protection given in GSGGe harness equipment etc. All Park Animals harness adjusted horizontally – Report sent to G.S. I/c F.S. & Gates R.E. H.Q. verbally. To All Transport inspected to G.O.C. Troops – Ellis.	Ellis

Army Form C. 2118.

WAR DIARY
or
INTELLIGENCE SUMMARY.
(Erase heading not required.)

Instructions regarding War Diaries and Intelligence Summaries are contained in F.S. Regs., Part II. and the Staff Manual respectively. Title pages will be prepared in manuscript.

Hour, Date, Place	Summary of Events and Information	Remarks and references to Appendices
15th November 1914 ST. OMER.	Inspected Transport & Gordon Highlanders - All Vehicles in good condition - Harness required minor repairs - Horses well looked after - 3 Men. A.S.C. sent to adv. 9 D of T. to LONDON Regt. 8 Horses returned by H.Q. & 3 prisoners - 1st Line - despatched by V.O.S.N.Q. unit to ABBEVILLE. 11 Injured Horses 1st Line sent back to Regiment - Detachment employed on received duties - Instruction given to Shoeing Smiths from Regiments - Inspected Transport of 4th SUFFOLK Regt - Vehicles in good order - required also several horses required shoeing - Previous report to Harness - carried out -	Spare
16th November - ST. OMER.	Spare Pte Purv - Sent to ORDNANCE. Officer here HARVE, the following Vehicles with by adva 9 D of T - S.H.O. S.B.S. Wagons. 2 Water Carts. drafts broken. 1 French Cart - reported by same. A Gunner reported B.H.Q. for 1st HERTFORDSHIRE Regt - despatched by Post Office van to Railhead, with order to join Supply Column proceeding to front, on Regiment have left to join Brigade at the front -	Spare
17th November - ST. OMER.	Paid Detachment 26 Cy Gre . 690 francs. Inspected Transport 4th SEAFORTH - Highlanders - Vehicles in good order - Pickaxe one . 4 Wheeled Civilian Cart - For carrying break to break or drag shoe ; also several bolts missing - Save Regiment one Complete Horse out ¢ ¢ in. harness sent to Adv. T. Depot - under 9 D of T. -	Spare

WAR DIARY
or
INTELLIGENCE SUMMARY.
(Erase heading not required.)

Army Form C. 2118.

Hour, Date, Place	Summary of Events and Information	Remarks and references to Appendices
15th November 1914 — St. OMER.	Instructed T.O. 4th Worcs fourteen report demands for horse shoes must needs, also stable management. Horses to be sent in for repair. 2 week leave 6 Sorders repaired. Bethune left by S. SCOTTISH RIFLES at HELFAUT reported to Staff Capt A. Reserve troops. Detachment received white knapsacks — also Parade Rifle instruction —	Epw
19th November — St OMER.	Visited 6th CHESHIRE Regt. instructed T.O. regards Parking Wagons & horses — sent Saddler & Shoey smiths to help — Reported to Staff Captain A.R. Troops — a certain Quantity of Ammunition left behind by 5th SCOTTISH Rifles. Horse Rugs W detachment have received from ORDNANCE base —	Epw
26th November St OMER.	Visited 6th CHESHIRE Regt Stable now impelled Saddlery Harness Por Pin deficient. Indent W Front Neils, taken but in to ORDNANCE. S & O. T.O. fifteen of Territorial units instructed to apply. Detachment Reviewed route march of minor discipline under 2nd DOWSE A.S.C.	C/Pw

Army Form C. 2118.

WAR DIARY
or
INTELLIGENCE SUMMARY.
(Erase heading not required.)

Instructions regarding War Diaries and Intelligence Summaries are contained in F.S. Regs., Part II. and the Staff Manual respectively. Title pages will be prepared in manuscript.

Hour, Date, Place	Summary of Events and Information	Remarks and references to Appendices
21st November. St OMER.	Went round with V.O. S.H.Q. inspected all Horses belonging to 2nd Royal Irish and A.S.C. details. Detachment paraded in Refrigeration —	Sgn
22nd November. St OMER	Visited Transport + Supply Park 6 & Jordan Highlanders 2 Wagons — Complete to the French Cart, under Lt DOWSE, Lt H.Q.S. 3rd Cavalry Div — Handed over and receipt obtained — Lt DOWSE A.S.C. returned on completion of duty. 5th Highland Light Infantry, left in the front. Detachment employed in General duties.	Sgn
23rd November. St OMER.	V.O. & Little joined for Army Reserve Troops — detained round S.H.Q. Escorts from Ordnance Ross arrived for detachment of horses. — Veterinary Escort received Detachment employed in General Fatigue work —	Sgn

Army Form C. 2118.

WAR DIARY
or
INTELLIGENCE SUMMARY.
(Erase heading not required.)

Instructions regarding War Diaries and Intelligence Summaries are contained in F.S. Regs., Part II. and the Staff Manual respectively. Title pages will be prepared in manuscript.

Hour, Date, Place	Summary of Events and Information	Remarks and references to Appendices
10 am 24th November 1914 ST OMER.	Visited 6 Londons at BLENDEQUES. Saw all horses etc " " Supplies " " " Shoeing required attention, informed T.O. General	
3.30 pm	Visited 6 Cheshire Regt – 4 Royal Welch Fusiliers.	
	16 P/Cattle Wagons left on horse at BLENDEQUES. Deepening Pan Mud fever – reported by V.O. attached to A.T.R. Troops. A quantity of Ration Biscuit was left behind by Man leaving – Staff Captain noted it, & returned to Supplies & O[ ] where necessary – 11 Conn Rngrs – 9 Green Howard Rations –	[signature]
25 November – ST OMER –	Visited 6 Londons at BLENDEQUES – a number of sick horses sent with V.O. – to find a sick horse left behind by 9th Highland Light Infantry – Detachment employed on local Transport work – Inspection of Boots and Clothing – 26 Coy ASC –	[signature]

Army Form C. 2118.

WAR DIARY
or
INTELLIGENCE SUMMARY.
(Erase heading not required.)

Hour, Date, Place	Summary of Events and Information	Remarks and references to Appendices
26 November 1914 St. OMER.	Went out to HAZEBROUCK to broken Wagon belonging to LEICESTERSHIRE Yeomanry, stationed at SYLVESTRE — and neighbouring farms. Wagon required minor adjustment to fore carriage & brake. This Unit is in possession of 3 Heavy Type Rifles Weapons. Not suitable for Cavalry work — reported by by T.S. Hood —	Form
27 November 1914 St. OMER.	On French Cart handed over to (Repeal Coy) returned from 8th Division N. IRISH HORSE - St. OMER. Parades to Welsh Fusiliers. ✓ 6 - Cheshire Regt. ✓ 4 - Seaforth Highlanders. ✓ Reported personally to Brigade Major — A Reserve Troops, recommends in horses to work at defences of Territorial units — Detachment employed on general duties.	Form

79

Army Form C. 2118.

WAR DIARY
or
INTELLIGENCE SUMMARY.
(Erase heading not required.)

Instructions regarding War Diaries and Intelligence Summaries are contained in F.S. Regs., Part II. and the Staff Manual respectively. Title pages will be prepared in manuscript.

Hour, Date, Place	Summary of Events and Information	Remarks and references to Appendices
November 28th St. OMER	Inspected Transport N.I.Irish Horse – On forming of 2 B.S. wagons. Ramper supplies. 2 followed SS wagons - 1 Maxim Cole – and Two French Carts – one wagon made up spare of 2 of T.9. M.T. Repairs carried out, Vehicle & harness – of "Iron-works Ruphandan" at field Freshan. – – – – – – – – – One broken wagon replaced English Town wt. for St. Sealote Nijfelander – Broken Wagon – sent down to A.T. Depôt LE MANS.	[sig]
November 29th St. OMER	Returned to A.M.T. Depôt – 5 Drivers English - returned from R.O. at [Holdingstrooms] – reported S.A. & one Groom. Inspected side horses of "Wheeler Freshan. – 6 Cheshire Regt. Ir. Suffolk Regt – made up deficiencies in Horses etc. before latter Regt. left for the front – Detachment employed in General duties.	[sig]

Army Form C. 2118.

WAR DIARY
or
INTELLIGENCE SUMMARY.
(Erase heading not required.)

Instructions regarding War Diaries and Intelligence Summaries are contained in F.S. Regs., Part II. and the Staff Manual respectively. Title pages will be prepared in manuscript.

Hour, Date, Place	Summary of Events and Information	Remarks and references to Appendices
30th November 1914 St-OMER-	At Reserve S.O.I. Troops - Inspected Transport of 6th CHESHIRE Regt. (9 Horse Slings) Rich and uninitiated - Pack Saddlery of all Pack Animals readjusted also several collars & horses. Instructor T.O. to have collars sent to Sergt Rawalla. In return - also to demand horse shoes - and horses required to be made up — 4th SUFFOLK Regt. Left in hot front - Vehicles & horses in good condition - a few suffering from cold - poor & indifferent, but one ox - also cup of a wheel. Detachment received in general duties - need discipline - Rifle instruction.	Epw

www.ingramcontent.com/pod-product-compliance
Lightning Source LLC
Chambersburg PA
CBHW081429160426
43193CB00013B/2235